God Talks
to
All of Us

Presented by
Kay Mielenz

Book Cover designed by LM Design Company of Colorado,
reachable at LMDesign5280@gmail.com.

Published by Divine Resources Inc.

Manufactured in Littleton, Colorado, USA

First Edition

Imprint: Divine Resources For All

ISBN: 978-1-955713-00-9 (paperback)

ISBN: 978-1-955713-04-7 (eBook)

Library of Congress Control Number: 2021914872

CONTENTS

ABOUT THE TRUE AUTHOR

I am the author of *God Talks to All of Us.* I am the Absolute Creator of all you see in existence. I do not judge one person as being more precious than any other. All are My beloved children. I am within each person's heart even though very few detect My presence.

I am not mysterious. I only seem mysterious because you do not understand what you are looking at. You see other people, animals, trees, oceans and all of creation on Earth and do not recognize that all are contained within Myself. I am ever-present within all of creation. All are divine offspring that have My essence within them. I am your parent, and I have decided that My children are in need of being taught directly by Me. I am not as I am commonly perceived, and all I ask of you, My children, is to be as I am.

ABOUT THE PRESENTER

Throughout her forties, Kay Mielenz developed an urgent desire to understand what life is really all about. She could not turn off her need to know. It did not make sense to her that life had no purpose other than experiencing one's youth, middle age, old age and then death.

At the age of 55, her life took a ninety-degree turn in a most remarkable direction. One day while quietly sitting in her favorite recliner, she began to detect a powerful presence blanketing her with extraordinarily high vibrations. Then she heard God's voice speaking to her for the first time. His voice was as clear as if He were standing right in front of her.

His divine voice said, "I am Creator God, and I am going to dictate My communication to humanity for you to record and distribute." She telepathically responded, "I hear you very clearly, but I do not have a good vocabulary, and I speak in simple sentences. This is not going to work."

God instructed her to acquire a sizeable notebook with which to record His dictation every afternoon, which she did. The following afternoon she dutifully sat down at her kitchen table with her fresh notebook, pen in hand, to see what would happen. To her amazement and supreme delight, Creator God began to speak to her.

Surprisingly, she heard His dictation with absolute clarity. She did not have to puzzle over the precise words He was saying. There was no second-guessing what she heard. She simply recorded what He said. After each day's session, she would read over that day's dictation to determine if it was rational, logical and cohesive. In every instance, it was. Over the three years of receiving daily dictation from Creator God, He accomplished His goal. He prepared Kay for the assignment He had in mind, to transmit His communication to humanity, although that task would not be forthcoming for nearly twenty years.

During the nearly two-decade lapse in time between Kay's training and the initiation of Creator God's communication to humanity through this book, she continued her dedication to assisting people who died under challenging circumstances. She developed the capability of aiding deceased people who stumble when faced with release from their physical body. Some deceased people go off course because they do not understand the mechanics of the natural transition intended to take place after dying. Kay documents the after-physical life goings-on, both positive and negative, in another book titled, *What It Is Like to Die and What Comes After*.

Kay is eager to share the insights God gave her so each of us can comprehend why we are alive and how we can shine the light of awareness on the importance of every single person without exception. When we understand the plan for our lives, we have a tremendous advantage. We become empowered to work towards our betterment, our children's betterment and the betterment of our planet.

ABOUT THE BOOK

God Talks to All of Us is a handbook of enlightenment for every person on Earth who wants to live the best life they can live, be the best person they can be, and contribute to the betterment of humanity and our planet Earth. Throughout this book, Creator God educates us. He teaches us by contrasting His traits and qualities with humanity's traits and qualities, and asks us to be as He is. He is our respectful teacher who wants us to place loving, supportive arms around each other and our planetary home.

INTRODUCTION

—

Creator God is calling all of us to attention. His purpose is to take the sand of delusion out of our eyes before it is too late for us to reverse the course we are on. As we look at our world today, we see our lesser qualities reflected back to us. Greed, selfishness, deception, and underhandedness are pulling morals and ethics down. These traits seem to be spreading to the point of becoming commonplace. How can adults teach children right from wrong when they themselves do not have high enough personal standards?

God Talks to All of Us gives us the understanding we need to make our world a better place for all people to reside. Creator God leads us on a course of self-awareness by comparing His attributes to our attributes. He discusses humanity's characteristics and compares our perceptions and behaviors to His own. Repeatedly, He encourages us to learn from Him and to be as He is.

Creator God sounds an alarm when describing our lack of commitment to the well-being of our planet and the generations to come. There is no denying the points He makes regarding the contamination of our food supply with chemical additives, how we utilize waterways, including the oceans, as dumping grounds and the poisoning of the air we breathe by pollutants expelled into the atmosphere. He warns us that we are heading for an environmental disaster of our own making on Earth as we sit on our hands doing little or nothing to stop massive ecological damage from occurring. He strongly makes the point that we are ultimately responsible for the well-being of our planet and our populations.

This direct communication from Creator God is our wake-up call. One cannot imagine how horrifying life on Earth will become if we continue to neglect our responsibility to safeguard our planet and if we continue to disregard the preciousness of every person on Earth. It is time for us to stand up as responsible citizens and shoulder responsibility for the well-being of our planet Earth.

CHAPTER ONE

WHO I AM

—⁓—

Creative intelligence combined with ever-expanding lovingness most clearly defines My being. I am the Absolute Creator of all you see in existence. I do not judge one person as more precious than another. All are My beloved children. I am within each person's heart even though very few detect My presence. I hold every person in My embrace, but very few detect My love flowing into them. I am clarifying how I am to correct misperceptions and to show you the way to model yourself after Me.

All of you are engaged in a personal experiment that is not apparent to you. Each of you is testing yourself to overcome character traits that fail to reflect your divine lineage. Earth is the testing ground where each individual repeatedly returns to challenge themself to rise to a higher standard of self-expression than they were able to demonstrate during their last incarnation.

Are you surprised that this is not the only time that you have been alive on Earth? If you knew the exact number of times, you would find it very interesting. My purpose for directly educating you is to help you understand why you are alive on Earth and what you can do to quicken your evolutionary progress.

I create from ideas, and each person originated as an idea in My mind. This may be hard for you to understand but consider how you create. The process always begins with an idea in your mind. The idea is your brainchild as so it is with Me. No thing comes into creation without being an extension of My divine creative process, which you have inherent within yourself as well. You are as I am, although this has been beyond your ability to comprehend.

We are as connected as a rain cloud is to the rain and as the ocean is to the fish within it. Without the rain cloud, the rain will not pour forth, and without the ocean, the fish will not reproduce. I am sustenance to all of you, but unlike the cloud or the ocean, I am invisible.

You do not perceive My presence as an addition to what you are seeing around you, so many of you do not think that I exist. Those that know Me personally, however, have ample proof of My existence. You may wonder how some people can know Me personally when others do not. I want you to understand that I do not favor some over others. Those who are determined to know Me personally and are willing to reach for Me internally open a path of connectivity.

I am extending Myself to each of you to invite you to draw closer to Me. My desire is for all of My children to know Me personally and to develop an interactive relationship with Me. I have given you life and individuality, making you different from one another.

I treasure your complexity and your loving nature when it shines through. I created you to be innovative, problem-solving, wise and determined to take care of yourself. I also created you to love one another as I love and cherish every one of you.

I understand how difficult it is to look at your world and comprehend that My presence is everywhere. Your perception of Me, if you have one at all, is most likely inaccurate. There are many mistaken convictions regarding where I am and what I require.

Most people who think they know what I am like are mistaken. It is common for some people to anoint themselves an expert in the field of God's requirements, but almost none of these people is offering anything other than what has been handed down to them from their predecessors, who did not receive the information directly from Me. Some of them are closer to being accurate than others, but overall, your world is awash in religious teachings that do not reflect My values.

Let Me tell you what My values are. I cherish every person without exception, even those who may not appear to merit My love because of terrible mistakes they have made. I value the well-being of every person, and I am pleased with those who give of themselves to ensure the welfare of other people. I am delighted when My children detect My presence within themselves. To those who are wise enough to look within themselves for evidence of My presence, I respond, but not right away. I make them earn the inner confirmation that I extend to those who truly desire to establish a personal relationship with Me.

> I am not mysterious. I only seem mysterious because you do not understand what you are looking at. You see other people, animals, trees, oceans and all of creation on Earth and do not recognize that all are contained within Myself. You have been looking for Me outside of yourself and outside of the rest of My creation. You have made Me separate when all of creation is contained within Me.

Have you ever thought about the thread of life that appears throughout creation? That thread is handed down from one generation to the next creating the experience of being alive on Earth. There is order built into the continuation of life. I am the cause that creates the effect, which you know as the continuation of life on Earth.

Do you witness the presence of the sperm fertilizing the egg? This is something that you know has occurred by the result it brings. Why then do most people think that I reside far away and am not present here on Earth, bringing about new life and supporting the cycles of living and dying? People who feel the rain on their faces are feeling My presence. I am unacknowledged while you enjoy My presence in every aspect of your existence.

You have not been successful in recognizing My presence right in front of you every day of your life. I do concede that I am baffling. I do not make it easy for people to know Me as I am without explanation. Only a few enlightened people instinctively know that I am ever-present within creation.

I decided not to remain reclusive anymore. There is a critical need right now for direct teaching that will enable everyone to learn directly from their Creator in order to realize truths that are not readily apparent.

Few people understand My true nature. I am an artist who creates worlds populated with people. These worlds have distinct characteristics, but all follow certain basic requirements. Your world, the world that exists on planet Earth, is the most rudimentary of all My created worlds.

On My other created worlds, every person works for the good of all, with few exceptions. Renegades do exist, but they are a small minority. The concept of working for the good of all describes My nature. I always love and cherish every one of My children, and I support them throughout their lives and thereafter.

Upon Earth, My true nature rarely shines forth unobstructed. People on Earth have yet to learn to expand the part of Myself that lies within their heart and to let that part lead them as they live their lives. My presence within each person can expand into a blaze of awareness that I am within him or her, giving clear, distinct proof of My existence. **No one can earn the expansion of My presence within them in any other way than by having love and compassion for all other people. If you want to detect My presence within you, you must love all My children.**

> Recognize that I am not complicated. My tenants are easy to understand, although not easily assimilated within human beings. People on Earth do not find it natural to be kind and considerate to all other people. They are more comfortable picking and choosing to whom they will extend themselves. I want all My children to start recognizing themselves and all other people as living, breathing, precious manifestations of Myself in human form.

I could not be closer to people since I am experiencing their lives right along with them. The part of Me that lies within each person senses, feels and understands what is going on within their life. I know everything, even things they will not acknowledge within themselves. Nothing is a secret to Me. I see goodness, and I see evil. I also see a lot of confusion that sends people off into actions that cause pain and sorrow.

Keep this in mind: pain and torment when caused by injustice, deceit or intolerance cause Me great sorrow. I suffer what My children suffer, and I know the truth behind their suffering. When one part of Me turns against another beloved part of Myself, I suffer doubly. I am disappointed in the person, who was too weak to act nobly, and I am feeling the injured person's pain, yet I love both of them equally.

As I witness My children, I am aware of the inconsistencies that govern their lives. Rarely do people steadily maintain high-quality behavior. They may be gracious and kind to certain people, but even then, not all the time.

People are selective when they interact with other people. Some they treat courteously. Some they ignore. Others they vilify. There is picking and choosing that goes on without a consistent right standard of interaction with all people.

> The simple explanation for this problem is that people evaluate the worth of other people by using their own flawed judgment. I see this happening everywhere at all levels of society. The human urge to devalue other people is contagious. Most people have at least some of this within themselves. No one would choose to be treated as many people treat each other.

Each person is a part of Me regardless of their perception of being separate from Me. I am the One that resides within every person. I am the One that created and holds within Me all of creation, which includes all living beings on Earth. I see all people as being sisters and brothers and hold none as more elevated than another. All are divine offspring that have My essence within them.

This is why it is unthinkable for one person to feel superior to another. Do your lungs feel superior to your heart or your fingers to your toes? Each is critically important, and this is how I feel about every one of My children. My love flows to every person, and I want everyone to accept all others as their beloveds.

I understand the challenges that life on Earth brings. The only certainty is My presence being within every person. I am knowable on a personal level, and I invite everyone to feel the stir of My presence within themselves. If you want to test if this is true, I invite you to follow My guidelines. First, take ahold of your mistaken thinking and correct it. Accept that I am in you and in every other person as well. Then try to feel My presence every morning upon awakening, every evening before sleep, and in between as often as possible.

When you reach for Me with a pure heart, you will feel the tingle of My presence, imperceptibly at first and then more detectably. When internal consciousness of My presence is awakened, this is just the beginning. I invite everyone to endeavor to intensify My presence within them by daily acting as My representative to every other person on Earth. This means holding dear every single person under all circumstances and modeling unconditional love and respect even under the most difficult conditions. I will be pleased with every person who accepts My invitation to awaken to who they really are and then become My active representative.

Nearly every person on Earth needs to be educated in the basics of proper behavior. As it is now, most people walk around as if they were wearing blindfolds, blindfolds that have some spots cut out, making them partially see-through. This gives each person limited perception because they are not seeing the whole picture.

One's particular cutouts allow them to see certain areas, which only give them partial awareness. However, they are convinced that their own view is the one accurate view because that is all that they themselves can see. Then when told that other people see things differently, they think that the other people are misguided.

This blindfold analogy is a description of what goes on all over your world. People do not see eye to eye because they all have their particular biases. They focus on what is important to them and simply ignore much of what may be important to other people.

I am the One who sees what is important to all people. I do not wear any kind of blindfold, nor do I favor one person over another. It is important for My children to throw away their blindfolds and acknowledge their biases. Completely removing those blindfolds is of paramount importance to accomplish as quickly as each person can. Nearly everyone is living with distortions of perception that invite conflict, misunderstanding or ill-treatment of other people. Yet, most are convinced of the rightness of their perception.

If it were not for one's own distorted thinking and other people's negative influences, human behavior would not be as disrupted as it is. It is common for people to copy other people, getting their ideas from what they see others do. People also tend to grab on to the influences that personally surround them as if they were a proper standard for all people. Hence, people that share the same views and objectives tend to stick together, and in some cases, they may strike out at others who they view as being inferior. Like attracts like, but this often leads to uncivilized behavior.

This is how factions begin: with strong will and conviction, that one's faction is superior and, in some cases, has the right to act against other people. Factions stir up trouble and can even result in wars. Rarely do people who are part of a faction that wants to take aggressive action against a group that displeases them create anything other than heartache for those people. Many of the most demeaning and disrespectful behaviors originate from people who have the conviction that they are superior to other people.

I do not fault the tendency that you have had to cling to beliefs and standards of the past that do not adhere to My principles. I understand the confusion that arises from not being able to discern truth from fallacy. I am determined to educate you to clear away disturbances that arise when the truth is overrun by that which runs counter to the truth. My clarifications may seem contrary to commonly accepted patterns of behavior and may require adjustment in your thinking.

Clearly, the world that enables the existence of life on Earth is on shaky footing now more than ever. If there ever was a time to be concerned about the future of the human race, this is the time. Guns and fighting do not bring a promising outlook for the future. Disregarding the well-being of the planet you live on will not ensure that she will continue to support your desire to remain as her guests.

Everyone is aware of the volatility on Earth and, although some people may not believe your planet has the capability to take corrective action, be forewarned. Calamities will arise, brought on by people's indifference to the disastrous effects of their actions that are destroying the well-being of their planetary home. It is almost too late to prevent your planet from rising up to demonstrate her power and her fury. Be forewarned and do everything in your collective power right now to take corrective steps to halt the aggravation that you press upon your planet.

Make a clearly defined effort to reverse the deterioration of your planetary home. Planet Earth's well-being is of extreme importance, beyond your ability to comprehend. All totaled, every act of support and consideration is not enough to overcome the many more acts of disgraceful treatment imposed upon your planet. Many of you are going to experience repercussions for the ill-treatment shown to her. I am very concerned, and you should be too.

People are used to living with problems, especially when they do not feel able to solve them. Small problems remain ignored until they become so big that ignoring them is no longer an option. This is the situation on Earth right now, and everyone will be impacted, even those who believe they will be able to avoid direct consequences. I am concerned about the viability of planet Earth and the human race over the next decades. There is an urgency to take responsible action now.

I understand the complexities of the problems that face the human race. Most people would like to pitch in and help solve the world's problems, but they feel insignificant within the greater picture. However, be advised that each person creates a world within themselves. Each person designs their personal world and lives within it. The greater world is the combination of all the personal worlds contributed by each person. One's personal world is their domain, and they can make it wholesome, contributing and of the finest code of ethics and behaviors.

What would the greater world be like if all of the personal worlds were determined to become pristine? People will not transform themselves unless they put forth great effort and determination. Personal motivation is the one force that has the potential to bring about revolutionary improvement within the microcosm and then the macrocosm. The housecleaning begins at home. This first step is essential. Take an inventory with clear vision that reveals one's particular shortcomings.

Once you identify your shortcomings, it is still necessary to go back and keep searching repeatedly until the spotlight of revelation discloses even those character flaws, which were either cherished or invisible. Most people have character flaws that are invisible to them but fully apparent to other people, and character flaws that they may be aware of but are proud to have, not recognizing the darkness in having them.

The shared world of everyone on Earth consists of all the personal worlds, most of which are wobbly. It is impossible for the greater world to transform without each of the personal worlds cleansing their attitudes, actions and, most of all, their thinking. What people do stems from how they think, what is in their minds.

Thoughts of anger and revenge lead to acts of brutality. Thoughts of selfishness lead to hoarding. Thoughts of denial shield one from the truth. Unmanaged thought processes create most of the problems that people have.

I recommend the clean slate method of self-evaluation. Instead of defending unwholesome aspects or failing to notice them altogether, lay them out in clear view but without emotional attachment or defensiveness.

Look at your unwholesome aspects as if they belonged to someone else, and then ask yourself three questions. If I were shopping, would I pay money to have this trait? Would I sell this trait to get rid of it? Would I pay someone to take this trait out of me? The answers will reveal how willing a person is to part with that part of themselves that is actually a weakness or a character flaw.

By following this exercise, if a person is completely forthright and honest, they will reveal what they need to concentrate on to wipe their slate clean of personal irresponsibility.

The whole is the sum of its parts, and this is evident when you consider all of the people on Earth. There must be a general cleansing of attitudes and actions within every person, done with the intention to contribute to one's own evolutionary progress and the world's betterment. It is true that there is a violent impulse within some people that ruins living conditions for a great number of others. These are the greatest violators of divine law upon Earth. They act against My will, some of them while using My name to justify their aggression against others.

People who exercise power over others, whether as elected representatives or dictators, military and law enforcement, heads of organizations of any sort, including religious, corporate or social organizations, and even within the family structure, all must hold themselves to a higher level of accountability. Being in a position of power is a place of temptation for weak and self-serving people when it should be an opportunity to shine forth to improve conditions for other people. Not many people have the high standard of working for the good of all, although this is exactly what your world needs most.

If people hold the same positive intentions for other people that they hold for themselves, your world will become a friendlier and safer place to live. Working for the common goal of transforming a conflict-laden world into a gentle and supportive place to exist has the potential to accomplish remarkable goodness instead of more conflict and adversity. Your world, as it is, could change with surprising rapidity. This is possible if all people unite with the common goal of doing their part, however large or small it may be, to smooth out conflict, to hold positive intentions to create only good for oneself and others, and to include all other people as being worthwhile and as precious as one would like to be to others.

Each person's world can change overnight if their focus redirects from being self-serving, especially when it is to the detriment of others, to becoming completely fair, honest and working for the good of all. This should not be hard to achieve; however, there is one step that precludes its effectiveness.

A person must set aside their aggressive instinct to ascend to the top of the ladder solely to be the top dog, the one who wields the power. The top dogs often are delinquents.

Being a top dog is a heady position in which to be, but know that those who have power over others automatically carry responsibility for safeguarding all those under their jurisdiction. Unfortunately, within the top dog mentality, there often exists the temptation to wield their power for personal ego infatuation and monetary gain, which leads to misery for those who have no other option than to follow the leader's dictates. Those who have power over others have the greatest opportunity to improve conditions for them yet may be the least interested in fulfilling this obligation.

Being the top dog is challenging to one's morals and ethics. Morals and ethics tend to fly out the window when there is position and power involved. Power grabs and the ability to dictate one's will to those who have no other option than to comply produce an exhilarating self-infatuation in some people. I know how this feels because I am within these people as well as those who are their patsies. Intolerable suffering is dished out wholesale while the top dog basks in its power, having no consideration for anyone other than himself.

People given power over others rarely see themselves for what they are. A high percentage of them are arrogant, controlling victimizers of common sense. Building an empire upon the backs of those who are unable to rebel against foul treatment or foul intentions creates moral decay and boatloads of karmic consequences raining down on the misguided top dogs.

Top dogs do not realize that they are not superior people. They let their power and what it brings justify their puffed-up self-perception. If they did not have power and position, they might view themselves more realistically.

No one is greater than anyone else is and certainly not greater because they have money or influence. What matters to Me are people who care about each other and are willing to do what they can to stand by another's side, especially during times of hardship or sorrow. The giants, in My estimation, are those who give of themselves with no thought of compensation. Your world has many of these giants who usually go unrecognized.

Having money in one's pocket does make life easier. The poor suffer the most. They have fewer opportunities to get ahead than those who are their equals but did not start out on such a low rung on the ladder. Being impoverished is a tough life circumstance to overcome and often made more difficult by employers who look down on impoverished people and treat them disrespectfully. A helping hand extended to an impoverished person means far more than it does to someone who has better options in life.

I would like all of My children to recognize that every impoverished person can be aided by several means. First, give respect and genuine caring. Then see what you can do to alleviate some of their problems, perhaps helping them make connections for employment or housing. If you have deep pockets, you can do more, but even those without deep pockets have the ability to work out potential solutions to some of their problems.

Your friendship will mean a lot to them and to Me. I am within every impoverished person as I am within you. The part of you that contains My presence grows increasingly larger with every act of loving kindness that you extend to others and especially to those who are downtrodden. Look at them as being Me in human form, for this is who they truly are.

I realize that people encounter differing life circumstances. Some seem to have it made from birth, while others cannot seem to get ahead no matter how much effort they put forth. Life does not treat all people equally, but helpful other people hold the key to making life less painful for those who are downtrodden. If people who have been held down because of life difficulties, either from birth or from aggravating life circumstances, were held in as high esteem as anyone else and offered opportunities, many would be able to extract themselves from at least some of their difficulties.

No one can give another a new life, but everyone can ease hardship and suffering through acts of compassion. Spending time with someone who needs comfort and reassurance is a gift that anyone can give. The time spent is worth its weight in gold to the recipient. Be on the lookout for ways to be an angel on Earth to your brothers and sisters who need a helping hand. Give what you have to give, be it transportation, economic support or just a warm hug.

What makes a successful life? This question has many answers depending on whom you ask. Certainly, having one's basic needs provided would be at the top of the list. The rich man needs more money than the poor man does. What is more than sufficient for the poor man is not nearly enough for the rich person. Some people measure success on their freedom to do and go where they please without restrictions. Some people shoot for the moon, and others are quite satisfied with a simple existence.

People are different, and I allow each to fulfill their dreams and desires by designing their own lives as best they can. This freedom to choose has an upside and a downside. When people are successful, they are pleased with themselves, even if for the wrong reason, such as attaining a position of power over other people. When peoples' lives do not pan out as they envisioned, they might be disappointed in themselves, although they may have accomplished a lot given the hurdles they had to overcome. Accurately judging success or failure in one's life requires a broader perspective than what typically comes to mind.

I will tell you how I evaluate a person's success during their lifetime. First, I look for improvement, improvement in attitude and perception. If a person had poor behavioral models as a child but throws off that negative influence as a teenager, and as an adult becomes an upstanding citizen, I give them an A+. This is one of the most difficult challenges to overcome, and not overcoming this challenge can result in wounding other people as well.

I honor this kind of success the most. This kind of success is not defined by money in the bank. It is defined by personal ethics and self-control. **I honor all people who treat other people fairly, respectfully and as their equal.** Only a small percentage of people hold true to this model of behavior.

Each generation passes on their prejudices and dysfunctions as if these were the family treasure. Then the younger generation follows along the same line if they do not use independent good judgment and self-control. Too often, generations of the same family repeat like robots what they heard and saw modeled to them as children. People have brains to think for themselves and direct their actions independently of what others influence them to do, and to be responsible for their personal standard of behavior.

Children, when they have good role models, are at a great advantage, and I expect them to live up to what they learned and further refine their attitudes and behaviors. However, even with good role models, this is not a slam-dunk. Without self-control and personal integrity, it is all too easy to be seduced by one's own distorted thinking or outside influences. Everyone is accountable for all their actions during their lifetime. Knowing this ahead of time, especially when one is young and starting to form their base of integrity, or lack of integrity, can make an evolutionary difference in how successful their life turns out to be.

A lot hinges on today's children. They are the ones who will bear the effects of what is happening on Earth now. The older generations have demonstrated that they do not know how to create peace on Earth and respect for all other people under all circumstances. It will be up to the younger generations to outperform their elders and accomplish what appears to be impossible.

When people are young, they have no idea that they are the shapers of tomorrow's world. Every young person deserves to have the very best life circumstances, and by this, I mean good, solid support from their immediate family, first of all, then also from their teachers and the entire rest of society. This generation of children who are young now will carry the burdens left over from their predecessors, and these burdens are significant.

Many of the world's challenges remain for future generations to resolve. The current generations have sat on their hands, observing catastrophe after catastrophe and doing nothing significant to right the overwhelming problems that humanity faces. The older generations and especially their governmental leadership behave as if these problems will resolve without a joint cooperative effort.

Do not deceive yourselves. You are used to closing your eyes to problems or skewing your thought processes to suit your purposes. Everyone needs to pull together and be honest with themselves in order to advance civilization. Good decisions and cooperative actions are required in order to tackle the myriad of problems that are piling up. Top dogs and ordinary people need to give up self-interest and indifference, which they must do before it is too late to reverse the damage already done.

The head-in-the-sand approach compounds problems, real problems that do exist and are crying out for remedies. The head-in-the-sand approach is no more effective than the ostrich's ploy to remain unseen. Solutions to problems require teamwork and cooperation, neither of which is the strong point of many who are in leadership positions. Too many of them prefer grandstanding and pushing personal agendas instead of working cooperatively to address the important issues that are their real responsibility.

Often, there is more effort put into tripping up the opposition than in working constructively with them. Everything could change if top dogs and those in leadership positions would stop thinking of their own self-motivated intentions and work for the good of all. Rational solutions to a myriad of problems exist because top dogs and those in leadership positions actually have the capacity to work for the good of all once they remove their oversized egos from the equation.

Much of the world's leadership is morally corrupt. Leaders who help themselves to excess while their constituents do not receive fair treatment do not deserve their position. Positions of leadership are often filled with power-mongers and not people who are truly dedicated to serving the needs of those under their jurisdiction.

> Gentler people who are good problem solvers would be the preferred leaders. They would be more likely to consider all people's needs and respond to them in the best ways possible that would not cause disruption for others. Satisfying diverse people is a chore, for many have conflicting preferences, and it takes wise leadership to make difficult decisions that keep in mind fairness to all. **Problem solvers are what the world needs -- active, wise and willing to take corrective action, problem solvers that do not hold personal gain as their motive.**

Corruption and disregard for others are rampant in your world. People think they are getting away with their misdeeds; however, all of their misdeeds are fully revealed to Me. I know what they are doing and what their intentions are.

Part of the cause of this disordered behavior is a common belief that people only live once. Those that have yet to develop an inner monitor that distinguishes right from wrong are often out to get all they can, in any way that they can successfully manipulate. Much of the world operates in this manner. It does not occur to people that they are fully accountable for all their actions while they are alive and that these actions will ultimately come home to roost.

After dying, each person reviews his or her life with perfect clarity. They see their whole life revealed and have to accept responsibility for their wickedness in particular. Evil actions have the direst effect on the newly deceased. What they did to disregard the well-being of other people will be in their face with no way to excuse their actions.

They have to experience the evil they brought to other people as if it were happening to themselves. This can be a brutal experience, but it is an effective educational tool. I give this warning: do unto others, as you would have them do unto you, for if you do evil to another, it will descend upon you as well.

Life is a series of experiences, and these experiences do not end when a person dies. Dying is just the end of physical life experiences for this lifetime. The human experience continues in the after-death state and feels similar to being alive on Earth but without a physical body. Physical bodies are not the only kind of bodies that people have. People mainly have spirit bodies, which is what sustains existence.

Once I create a person, that person is Mine forever. They keep experiencing different realities that I have caused to exist either on Earth or in other places. I am the Creator God who holds all in My loving embrace. All of My creation is part of Me and always will be. This is difficult to comprehend for people who think they cease to exist after they die. They will live forever as part of Me.

All people build goodness within them as they live lifetime after lifetime. Each person builds up a storehouse of refined behaviors as they maneuver through each life experience making good choices and poor choices. Their life review helps them plan the course for their next life experience, with the intention of passing the tests that they failed in past attempts. Through this process, each person slowly takes on attributes that I consider to be of utmost importance. When a person reaches an elevated state of development, they may exercise the option of experiencing other placements.

Earth is the least desirable place to experience because, in general, the people that live on Earth are beginners. There are certain basic behaviors that are difficult for people on Earth to establish within themselves. Their instincts are to act selfishly instead of magnanimously.

On Earth, people tend to feel that it is every man for himself, and they are out to get as much as they can. A person's principles are easy to compromise, and the other person's problems are just that. Shared responsibility for the good of all is in short supply, even though that is what builds character within each person. Earth is a place of feeling separate from other people, instead of a place where people are born with open hearts for all of their brothers and sisters.

When one can pass the test of holding **all** people in a loving embrace, they have passed the final examination and are free to occupy more evolved parts of My creation. I cannot have beginners from Earth disrupting more evolved planetary communities. Every person has the ability to work their way up to the most elevated levels by constantly evolving every aspect of their self-expression.

My divine plan calls for each person to ultimately realize that they are replicas of Myself and to take My characteristics as their own. I want everyone to become divinely developed and to enjoy existing in the same rarefied atmosphere that I reserve for those who can attain My state of perfection.

Earth is the beginning point, and it is the elementary school of the universes. Most of the people who live on Earth have restricted vision. They only see as far as their own well-being and think that others do not matter as much as they do. This is the primary hurdle to overcome, and until they overcome this hurdle, Earth's students will continue to return, repeatedly displaying the same behaviors and wondering what life is all about.

Life on Earth is not evolving as quickly as I had hoped. Most people have the instinct to overrate their own importance and to underrate the importance of others who they judge to be of lesser value. There is a lot of self-absorption and unhappiness.

Many people live in a circle of misery. They go round and round, dealing with their problems and not being able to catch a breath. Problems would not exist if it were not for what people are supposed to be learning from them. The best way to work through the problems that life hands out is to strive to comprehend the lessons presented. Problems offer opportunities to advance one's self-development.

Lives that seem long, in reality, are not. Time is an illusion that does not exist anywhere else than Earth. On Earth, I mercifully limit the duration of people's experiences. Since the challenges are significant, I do not allow lifetimes to extend indefinitely.

When a person is born, they bring along an agenda for their lifetime. Some agendas are exceptionally ambitious, requiring an extended lifetime to complete. In most cases, the best work on self-advancement comes in old age, when people are more likely to become introspective if they have not been before. Some people finish their agendas quickly and do not choose to remain. The bottom line is that people have intentions for their lives, and they may or may not remain once their intentions have been satisfied.

Knowing that people are living on Earth for particular reasons ought to give every person an urge to become introspective. Hidden within plain view are one's life lessons but, if you do not play detective, you will miss noticing them. Even if one does not figure out the reason for certain problems or disruptions in their life, going through those challenges are going to edge one closer to learning the intended lesson.

Human life is intended to advance personal behaviors and attributes and to reform each person into a gentler, more sympathetic and understanding representative of My presence on Earth. Be aware that individuals can quicken the pace considerably if they work at it. Conscious awareness of your thought processes helps to uncover the true picture of what you are creating in your life. Total honesty with no need to distort intentions will show anyone who is willing to look exactly how they are creating their life. Taking this perceptive approach over time will reveal much that lays hidden, which a person needs to correct.

Every life has challenges, even those that appear not to be as heavy as other people's lives. **People do not come to Earth for a holiday.** Lives that appear to be glamorous have as many or more lessons to learn as simpler lives. Do not make the mistake of thinking that some people get a free ticket. Sometimes those that look the most as if they are leading easy lives are really leading lazy lives in which they waste the opportunity to raise themselves up to a higher level of self-expression.

Evolution on Earth is a slow process made slower when people do not care to exert themselves to become better than they are. The lazy way out only sends the person back through the revolving door to experience physical life repeatedly. This will continue until they finally grasp the need to revolutionize their self-presentation and bring it up to a high enough standard for them to graduate from the school of Earth.

Being alive on Earth comes with certain responsibilities. No one receives the list of responsibilities when they are born, so there is understandable confusion. My aim is to give everyone a clear understanding of what My intentions are for every person's development. **My aims are the same for everybody.**

I want every person to realize that they have responsibility for refining their attitudes and behaviors to reflect My presence within themselves.

I want every person to cherish themselves and all other people reflecting My personal feelings for every human being.

I want everyone to build a world based on trust instead of deception, sharing instead of hoarding, respecting instead of denigrating, and embracing instead of destroying each other.

Let truth and consideration prevail and lead to greater compatibility, each with every other person.

CHAPTER TWO

HOW I AM

—

My heart overflows with love for each of My children and for all of My creation. Every person is precious to me, and I am eager to lead you, My beloved children, forward in your evolutionary progress, which will advance your personal well-being and the well-being of your planetary home. Direct communication is My preference since roundabout methods typically escape humanity's comprehension.

There are many notions in people's minds regarding how I am, mainly because you attribute to Me characteristics that are similar to your own. You have thought of Me as being harsh and critical, demanding and punishing. I am not as I am commonly perceived, and all I ask of you, My children, is to be as I am.

Your world is in dire need of redirection. Most of you are going the wrong way. Instead of growing in ever-expanding love, your world reflects a pulling-in of loving instincts. In many instances, you utilize your creative intelligence to harm other people as you set out to make your way in the world. I am giving you notice that I did not create you to go around harming other people. I created you and gave you individuality to prove to yourself that you can be exactly as I am.

Patiently, I wait for more of My children to direct their attention to using their creative intelligence to relieve the pain, hardship and suffering of other people. Very few of My precious children focus their direct attention on finding ways to help other people. I understand that your lives are busy, but what is all that busyness producing? More for some and still not enough for others.

When you look in the mirror, you see how you look as your individual self. My mirror is different from yours. When I look in the mirror, I see each of you individually, and I see whether you are displaying yourself as My direct offspring.

> It is not apparent to you that you can be the same as I am. You have tremendous potential to emanate loving kindness as you apply your creative intelligence. I want you to uncover the beauty that lies within yourself. What you see in the mirror is not all that defines you.

My determination to instruct you springs directly from the general state of affairs on Earth. Many well-meaning people cause disruptions for themselves and for others without having any idea that they were instrumental in causing the problems. People's tendency to look outward instead of inward carries a built-in bias that attaches responsibility for conflicts to the other person. No one enjoys taking responsibility for something that has gone awry. Rarely do you see a person stand up and say, "I may be at fault here."

A most character-building trait to develop is becoming watchful to perceive the integrity and consequences of your actions. It is easy to charge ahead expressing oneself without recognizing when you are being mildly offensive or even tremendously hurtful. People tend to step on other people's feelings and rights with disregard.

Do not pretend that you are an angel when others would never perceive you as such. In addition, do not think that you are the king of the mountain. People who spend their lives only looking outward instead of turning inward to analyze themselves will not develop accurate self-perception.

Be yourself. Use the talents and gifts you were given but in a good way. Express yourself genuinely and always with respect for other people. Never rate yourself higher than any other person, for truly, I love everyone the same.

> Be secure that you as an individual are important to Me. You may think, "How does God even know me? There are so many people. How can He keep track of all of us?" I assure you that I do keep track of all of you, and I will tell you this: I am most delighted by people who keep their hearts wide open to all of My other children.

Only a few know how tender and loving I am from their personal contact with Me. I invite all of you to reach for Me, and in time I will give you the satisfaction of feeling My presence within you. You may think that personal contact with your Creator God is an impossibility. You are reading proof that this contact can become a reality.

I am eager to have a close, personal relationship with every one of you. If you do not believe this is possible, I challenge you to move toward this goal and see what happens. Be forewarned. I always know what your objectives are, and I only respond to those with pure hearts and pristine intentions. It is up to you to initiate a personal relationship with Me.

My heart fills with love but also with sadness for every person on Earth. Even those who are close to Me, whose hearts are filled with selfless love for other people, are not immune from suffering caused by man's inhumanity to man. Kindness and caring that should be flowing out to all remain reserved for only a few.

People pull in their impulse to do good as if it were dangerous to use too much of it. Yet, everyone benefits when people are good to each other. The elevated feelings of well-being that burst forth within people when they assist others are reason enough to go out of your way to lend a helping hand.

Those that give, receive. Instead of losing something of value, the gates of good fortune swing open for generous-spirited people. Their good fortune begins with feelings of worthwhileness that envelop them and make them feel good about themselves.

If you want to feel good about yourself, do something beneficial for someone else. It can be as simple as holding a door open for someone who is in need of assistance. Can you imagine how your world would be uplifted if every single person valued helping other people?

I cannot overemphasize how important it is to contribute to the well-being of others. Giving love, time, attention and support to those who grace your lives is of paramount importance. One generation creates the next. Each generation is beholden to those who preceded them. Plant the seeds of all the good qualities a person can have within your families to grow and flourish during the current generations and those that will follow.

Parents are responsible for teaching their children. I am your parent, and I have decided that My children are in need of being taught directly by Me. I am going to shine the light of My reasoning on current attitudes and actions that are disturbing respectful, peaceful interactions between people. Mistaken perceptions within humanity lead to widespread befuddlement instead of precise clarity when it comes to the question of how people can get along with each other instead of butting heads.

I invite you to become educated and to apply this education in your everyday lives. The more determined and successful you become, the more you will understand at a deep level the absolute simplicity of what I ask of each of you. I am asking you to be as I am.

There are some people who know Me as I am, but most of you have notions about Me that are not accurate. I do not judge. I observe. I observe the progress you make as you go about living your lives. I see your weaknesses, your deficiencies and the effort you put into overcoming them. I see your misconceptions.

I see how you capitalize on doing what you can to boost yourself over other people. I see your need to prove that you are worthwhile, and I see how you go about convincing yourself of your worthwhileness. I understand your underlying need to feel successful in worldly ways.

I have given you a mysterious path, one that I did not clearly define. I set you down upon the Earth, each in your own set of circumstances. I did not include direct instructions for you to follow, hoping that you would catch on to My principles naturally and show Me that you can be as I am. Slowly, humanity has progressed, and some of you have advanced to the point of being able to detect My presence within yourselves, but I am getting impatient. Underhanded behaviors, and even confusion over what is and what is not underhanded, muddle the forward progress of humanity.

Do not think that I cannot know you personally. My beloveds, I am aware of your intentions even when you mask them to yourself. I see beyond your self-deceptions.

I advise you to gather your courage and become determined to be honest with yourself. You are on your way to recognizing that you are a part of Me. When you deceive yourself that you are behaving with integrity when you really are not, you push yourself away from being able to recognize who you truly are.

I decided to teach you at this time to prevent the continuation of blatant disregard for the well-being of many of your sisters and brothers on Earth. Everywhere, but in certain areas more than others, some people are forced to absorb the brunt of other people's cruelty. Keep in mind that it only takes a few evil doers to destroy positive life circumstances for many people.

Cleansing the Earth has as much to do with depriving evildoers of their base of support as does cleansing oneself of primitive attitudes and behaviors. A two-tiered approach is required. Disable personal wrong thinking and acting, and disable any kind of leadership that espouses treachery against any human being.

People are suffering, and many of those who are compassionate want to help, but often they do not know what steps to take. Nothing less than educating all of My children will bring about far-reaching, lasting improvements. Without an education that everyone can understand and immediately apply to himself or herself, there is little hope that the bubbling caldron of ill-treatment of other people will cease.

Allow Me to educate you. Take advantage of My teaching and use it, not only to stem the tide of hurtfulness within humanity but also to help you draw closer to Me. When you love one another and act with tenderness and compassion, you draw close to Me. When you put your arms around someone in need and help them, you are extending yourself as My direct representative. I need all of you to collaborate with Me to uplift those who are living with severe life challenges, including pain and sorrow, either in your own backyard or around the globe.

Your world is in a muddle right now partly because there has not been a universal standard of decency followed by all people. Those who acknowledge My existence but spend their time turning people against one another are in need of remedial education. People who live for themselves alone and do not care about what happens to other people are missing the enrichment that comes with extending one's self to uplift and support another person. Why would you choose not to give Me the gift of caring for one of My own beloveds?

I am dedicated to educating all of My children. Every person on Earth is a child of mine, but it is difficult to find anyone who is well educated in that, which is of prime importance to Me. I am offering this direct education to every one of you in the hopes that you will become roused to recreate yourselves in My image.

You can only become educated if you maintain an open mind. You must be willing to set aside those beliefs and behaviors, which conflict with My teachings. Be sure that you do not instinctively screen out My instructions that make you feel uncomfortable. The points that cause you to have a squirmy feeling inside are likely to be your deficits. Do not overlook the signal that something requires your attention and your correction.

It should be obvious that everyone has some personal behavioral flaws. There is not a person on Earth who is exactly like Me. Your goal is to inform yourself about your flawed perceptions and attitudes with the intention of eliminating them to the greatest extent possible at this time.

Keep in mind that long-established faulty traits and behaviors do not disappear overnight. Most likely, you will have to put considerable effort into shrinking them bit by bit. As you undertake this daunting task, it may help you to know that nothing you do or have done in the past will ever cause Me to cast you aside. You are a part of Me. I reside within each of you, and each of you resides within Me.

I am your teacher, your father, your mother and your conscience. I am clarifying My principles to give you a firm foundation from which to elevate your understanding. Much confusion exists over what constitutes acceptable attitudes and behaviors, with relatively few people using the same criteria that I apply. Most people give themselves higher marks than they truly deserve.

Consider yourselves family members. All of you are related to each other, even though you may not bear a family resemblance. I am the commonality within all of you. I am the spark of life that gives you animation, self-identity and perception. I trigger the instinct to express yourself individually. However, I hide Myself to give you the challenge of loving and accepting each other as beloved family members.

Now I am doing what I have not done before. I am schooling you Myself. I am going to explain your weaknesses and failures in the hopes that you will recognize when you are headed in the wrong direction, away from Me, instead of becoming closer to Me. I am going to point out My preferences for your behavior, so you will have no excuse for not improving yourselves. You may not have known better before reading this instruction manual, but after reading, you will know better and will lose any excuse for not improving your attitudes, behaviors and the worthwhileness of your lifetime on Earth.

Throughout history, few people have known how I truly am. Common perspectives are often based on conjecture, misunderstanding and outright made-up falsity. I realize that much confusion arose from historical religious interpretations that took on the pretext of being absolute truth.

Absolute truth does not change and is valid for all generations of all people for all time. No matter how deeply you respect and believe what your religion teaches, you need to have confirmation that those teachings reflect My standards. My standards are applicable to the entire human race and not merely for one group or another.

Religious practices do not displease Me as long as they incorporate the absolute truth of how I really am. For example, as I have already indicated, I do not favor one person over another. All are equally precious to Me. Historically upon

Earth, some religious groups considered themselves to be My chosen ones as if I love some of My children more than the rest.

Some religious groups who feel superior to other religious groups at times have brought havoc upon those who follow different spiritual practices. Under the banner of religious righteousness, cruel treatment of innocents prevailed. Stay away from any spiritual practice that brings harm to any living creature and never justify religious righteousness. I value people who love other people without placing judgments or demands upon them.

I extend Myself to all of you regardless of what your prior beliefs have been. I want to make it clear that what really matters most when you are alive on Earth is to model yourself after My nature. I am ever-expanding goodness, rightness and benevolence. If you turn in My direction and reach for Me, I will extend Myself to you.

Many people yearn to be close to Me, but they do not understand what draws Me near and strengthens our bond. I am willing to teach you. Are you willing to know Me as I am? Are you willing to become like Me? Are you willing to undertake a course in becoming as I am?

I invite you to learn from Me what every person needs to know. I will lead you page by page through the rest of this book. Then by the end, you will understand that without a doubt, there is a better way for you to express yourself, which you will most likely be inclined to embrace.

This course begins by encouraging the examination of your established beliefs with an eye toward comprehending if these positions reflect My values and if they positively influence your evolutionary progress. Question whether or not your beliefs support your progression as an intelligent, rational and responsible person, one who reflects My standards. Questioning yourself is essential. Those who do not examine the worthiness of their beliefs and behaviors with an eye focused on personal improvement are in jeopardy of passing down to younger generations the same kind of wrong thinking and behaving that is playing out in the world today.

It is of utmost importance that you clearly understand that all of you, without exception, are My precious children. The color of your skin, your nationality, your religion, if you even practice a religion, none of these distinguishing characteristics makes any difference to Me whatsoever. What matters to Me is how you treat each other, how you respect and care for one another and how you go out of your way to help another who is in need.

I am reaching out to you now to straighten the mess that is apparent in your world of chaotic discord that separates and antagonizes people who appear to be different or those who are too weak to strike back against mistreatment. I am standing up for all those people who have taken the brunt of dominance by ruthless individuals, as well as those who are disregarded as the faceless masses of people who desperately need to be recognized and held as being important. All are My children. However, as is readily apparent by the suffering and the inequities that are broadly evident, My children do not consider themselves to be sisters and brothers.

Since I am your Creator God and all of you are My children, this makes each of you a sister or brother to all of My other children. Right now, the Earth family is in major disarray. Greed, dominance and disregard for the well-being of other people bring heartache for those who are mistreated.

There are not enough kind, loving, compassionate people willing to devote themselves to alleviating the suffering of others. The greatest fulfillment in life comes from helping other people, and those who do not take this opportunity experience a nagging emptiness inside. A great number of people seek meaning in their life. Setting one's sights on becoming a supportive, helpful person, who especially delights in uplifting the downtrodden, is the surest way to develop joyful feelings of enhanced self-worth.

I see what lies within the hearts and minds of all My children. I see the struggles they go through, and I see what is most rewarding, character building and uplifting to everyone who has an open mind and a big heart. The most effective way to nurture oneself is to create a positive impact for another person. Your soul expands every time you place another person's well-being at the forefront of your intentions.

There is a tremendous need for all people to be directly educated by Me. Although you may be reading this on paper or on a computer, or hearing an audio version, know that I am talking directly to you. Each of you is My responsibility to educate and, since roundabout methods have not worked so far, I am taking the direct approach. I admonish you to pay close attention and apply My teachings.

I will lead you to gain a clearer understanding of the importance of knowing yourself accurately and identifying those aspects of yourself that are throwing you off the higher course for your life. If you take My words to heart and put effort into self-analysis and then into revising mistaken attitudes and behaviors, you will begin to know yourself at a deeper level. You will start to feel yourself as you truly are in your pristine state without the confusions and delusions of earthy perspectives.

First, recognize that you are a chip off the old block. You are a part of Myself regardless of your past history. Inherently within you lies the capacity to go back to the way you were when you were still attached to Me. All of you were a part of Myself before I sent you out to experience as individuals what it would be like to feel separate from Me.

Do you not sometimes experience a lonely emotional state when you are quietly alone? You may wonder why you feel this way. You may have a deep longing for something that is not identifiable. No one on Earth is an island unto his or her self. Everyone still carries their attachment to Me embedded deeply within them and usually covered over with the joys, the delights, the drama and the trauma of everyday life.

Even though you are an individual person, part of Myself always resides within you. This gives you the innate capacity to remain part of Myself even though you appear to be completely severed from Me. Truly, I am within every one of you.

We are interconnected and always will be. I am consciously aware of all that you do, as I am experiencing through every one of you. When you are kind to another, you are being kind to Me. If you treat another person cruelly, I feel the pain they feel. There is no dividing line between us.

Your world is full of illusion, and since you cannot remember where you came from or why you are here now, you accept the illusion as reality. Each of you is indestructible. Your true essence never dies. Yes, your physical body will be discarded at some point in this evolving experience that you are embedded in right now, but the you-ness in you will always continue on experiencing, evolving and growing closer to identifying yourself as an integral part of Myself.

I am omnipresent, which means that I am everywhere. I am in all of creation. The sun, the stars and the planets are parts of Myself. Every person of every color and every physical likeness is Myself in a different form.

I am enjoying being in all of creation on your planet, as well as, in all creation in other realms of experience other than the one that is currently obvious to you. Your experience here is narrow in scope since Earth is the primary school of the cosmos. Most people on Earth are beginners, as they have not yet advanced to exemplary levels of behavior.

Eventually, you will recognize My goodness within yourself. Then, if you have not already, you will recognize that all people have My presence within them even when they are not aware of this themselves. Most likely, these concepts are new to you, and you may doubt what I am saying. If you examine your behavior and the behavior of other people, you would have little basis with which to come to these conclusions yourself. Humanity desperately needs divine assistance to understand the purpose of their lives and to correct their thinking, their attitudes and their behavior.

Your world is becoming a precariously dangerous place to live and evolve oneself. Without insight and instruction as to how to improve the outlook for the future of your world, the dynamics that are in place will lead to greater and greater chaos. I advise everyone to take a hand in the gentling of life on Earth by beginning to evaluate and improve his or her own perceptions and behaviors. Start by envisioning oneself and all others as divine offspring and then honoring all as such. This is the best first step to take in the elevation of perceptions and attitudes, which are necessary on Earth.

It is natural for Me to keep expanding. As I spin-off parts of Myself into creation, I am increasing My experience of being conscious within My creation. My nature is an energetic mass of loving intelligence that experiences individuality through My little selves that I released into apparent separateness. In other words, I am the thought that creates and you, My children, are the manifestations of My determination to extend Myself into physical form.

I am giving you information that is beyond the scope of one's ability to perceive for them self. Do not let this bother you or cause you to stop and say, "This cannot be true. This does not make sense to me." Continue with reason as your guide and determine if what follows in the rest of My communication leads you to grasp that My presence truly is within you.

I am not a God of your descriptions or imaginings. I do not sit in judgment. I am not vengeful or vindictive. I am infinitely loving and accepting of all people. I am determined to boost every person's well-being by providing the insight necessary to duplicate how I am within yourselves. I challenge every one of you to become infinitely loving and accepting of all people. When you reach this pinnacle of achievement, you will be qualified to go on to discover and experience other worlds.

You cannot be separate from Me. All creation is interconnected. The feeling of separation comes from the illusion of separateness and the forgetfulness that comes with being a human being living on Earth. I acknowledge that I have made it difficult for you to remember who you really are. I want you to discover this for yourselves by accessing the inherent divinity within you and displaying it within your daily lives. Put forth discipline and effort to become as kind, loving and helpful as you can be to each of your sisters and brothers on Earth.

I created worlds for you to explore. Earth is not the only one. I want you to prove yourself on Earth, so you will qualify for experiences that are even more spectacular. Look upon your time on Earth as the beginning point of an endless stream of opportunities.

Now is the moment in time that counts the most. It is now that you can take action to expand your knowing of yourself as you truly are and learn from Me what it will take to evolve into a more elevated self-expression. I am going into detail within the chapters ahead to help you to perceive yourself clearly and become a powerful force for good.

I invite you to use this communication of Mine as your modern-day Bible or Koran. Integrate what I am teaching you and put this knowledge to work immediately. Your world needs your commitment to raising standards and behaviors on Earth. You cannot leave it to other people to pave the way for universal respect and peaceful interactions to become common behavior. It is going to take a dedicated commitment from every person to transform your world into one of genuine respect and caring for all other people.

It will take both personal effort and group effort to rid the Earth of negative interactions. I invite everyone to participate in redesigning life on Earth according to the model that I am giving you. Mimic Me. Be as I am. Use Me as your guide. Follow My instructions and apply My teachings to yourself. I am opening a door for you to gain an understanding of how humanity can bring about a turnaround in the discordant atmosphere on Earth.

CHAPTER THREE

A MIRROR

I did not intend for your residence upon planet Earth to be a vacation experience. Earth is a training ground for everyone regardless of his or her level of personal development. Even saintly people have some deficiencies to challenge them.

People who choose not to capitalize on their opportunity to advance themselves typically feel satisfied with their self-presentation and give themselves an undeserved pat on the back. I am disturbed when a great many people give themselves a light and cursory self-review, if any at all, similar to being enrolled in a school in which it does not matter if one passes or fails because no one really cares. People squander many lifetimes without instilling notable improvements before the person's hourglass of opportunity runs out.

Before your time expires, I suggest that you get to know yourself as you truly are without the ego's need to gloss over deficiencies. The list of potential shortcomings is enormous, with most people having several that are predominant and worth addressing in order to transform their self-presentation. I am not asking that everyone perform a complete overhaul of his or her entire catalog of deficiencies. I am only asking that each person choose their most ingrained, against common decency, behavioral aspects to address, at least in the beginning.

Pockets full of money do not create a superior person, nor does a long list of accomplishments unless they contribute to the welfare of others. It is satisfying to apply one's talents and attributes to express oneself, but these gifts do not make one person inherently more valuable than another. Everyone needs to consider themselves equal to, but not greater than, anyone else and to use this as their self-appraisal.

From My perspective, observing people looking down on other people is ridiculous. I see through the masking of character deficiencies and the false measuring devices that people use to project superiority over other people. I see people walking down the street with their noses in the air as they pass by other people who have their noses in the air, each feeling superior to the other.

There is a common, self-serving tendency to overrate oneself and underrate the other person using criteria such as position, power, skin color, physical beauty, religious persuasion or lack thereof, or any other of an unlimited number of concocted criteria. None of these criteria is valid within My mind. As far as I am concerned, people are equal to every other, regardless of their personal characteristics, and if I do not discriminate against anyone, there is no justification for anyone to discriminate.

> I am waiting for everyone to learn this most basic point. Until non-discrimination and respect for every person become the universal behavior code, derogatory judgments will continue to conjure disrespect between people. At the most basic levels, from the family to the neighborhood, to the city, state and country level, every person on Earth must adjust their tendency to see themselves as better than, or less than, other people.

Frequently people who regulate countries or organizations can be prime examples of ordinary people who, when given the power to govern, pump themselves up with their perception of superiority. With this mindset, it can be tempting to take action that will undermine the well-being of some of those they are responsible for governing, as well as those who they may designate as enemies. The presumption of superiority eats away at the moral fiber of a person and clouds their judgment. As I explain these concepts, consider how they apply in the world of your time and prior to your time.

As you go about living your day-to-day life, keep in mind that you are creating a record of your life. What you do while you are alive does not disappear. One of the first things you do after dying and arriving within the heavens is to watch the movie of your life. All the golden moments that you cherish will be in plain view, as well as the moments that will be painful to watch because they display the disappointing side of yourself.

Everyone sits in judgment of how they lived their life. Each person views and assesses how their actions affected other people and themselves. They witness their entire lives as if they were watching a moving picture show of their life, clearly displaying what they did that hurt themselves or other people.

They view all their honorable actions and the joy and happiness they created during their lifetime. Everyone witnesses themself as they truly were, and what most people find is that they did not have a very accurate self-assessment as they were living their physical life. They become cognizant of their wrongdoing, mistaken attitudes and shameful behaviors along with everything about their self-expression that is pleasant to acknowledge.

My reason for informing you about the movie of your life is to let you know that what you do when you are alive does not disappear. This record will come back to demonstrate how you performed during your current lifetime. So be forewarned. Make sure that you are not creating a record of your life that will bring shame and a heartsick feeling to you when it is too late to implement corrections.

Now is the time to take a personal appraisal of your self-expression. Be honest with yourself. Recognize your beliefs and actions that will ultimately fill you with disappointment in yourself after you pass from your physical body if you do not improve on them while you are still alive.

Life is not a dress rehearsal. Life is the main event, and you cannot go back and change a poor performance. You have to give the best that you have within you right now, for this is the main event that will stand as recorded.

There is another aspect to your life review. Since it clearly points out your deficiencies, you understand what your weaknesses were when you were alive, and you realize what you need to do in your next lifetime to overcome them. However, overcoming one's unethical attitudes and actions that were inherent within oneself during their past lifetime is not a slam-dunk.

People tend to repeat past tendencies and, when their next lifetime begins, the agenda that they set out to accomplish will not automatically pop into their minds. Unless they receive some help, such as being born to parents who place a high value on educating their children in morals and ethics, the person is likely to repeat the behaviors that they intended to abolish.

It can be very difficult to distinguish the higher road in life, especially when good role models and direct instruction are lacking. I am endeavoring to make the playing field even by giving all of My children direct instruction. I am educating you on the principles that are essential for you to incorporate within yourselves. I am giving you what you know to be true when you are between lifetimes delighting in the atmosphere of the heavens and planning to recreate that same atmosphere on Earth when you return.

Take My instruction and go forward to implement My principles and way of being within yourself. I am your wise parent who is instructing you and helping you to be the best person that you can be. I dearly love every person. My intention is to further your evolutionary progress and to teach you to love as I love.

Whenever a person is in a position of authority, they have a moral obligation to act with wisdom, fairness and for the good of all. Arrogant or self-serving people are not ideal choices to fill positions of authority. Good leaders come from the ranks of those who have the impulse to serve others without trying to elevate themselves in the process. Humble people who are intelligent, fair-minded and reasonable make the best leaders. People prefer having them in charge, and they are far more likely to act for the good of all.

Corporations, governments and international federations would benefit if people, who tend to manipulate through means such as power-grabbing, muscle-flexing and deceit, were overlooked for leadership positions. Qualified and capable people may be routinely passed over for leadership positions because they are not flashy and do not improvise to appear to be what they are not. I am all-knowing. Contrived tricks and displays do not fool me.

Much of what goes on in politics is phony baloney. I am referring to the maneuvering for position and power, finding others to align with to advance one's position but sometimes at a sacrifice to morals, ethics and to the public good. Most politicians start out with positive ambitions and ideals but too often, they end up sacrificing their ideals to further their ambitions and to hang onto power. You may say that is just the nature of politics, but it does not have to be. If all politicians worked for the public good, instead of putting their personal or party's agenda ahead of the public good, even with differing opinions, better legislation would emerge.

I hold those in positions of leadership to higher standards than they generally hold themselves. When someone is making decisions that affect the well-being of My precious children, I insist that they act wisely and without dishonesty or self-interest that undermines the well-being of those they are responsible for governing.

This should not be difficult, and it is not when self-interest is not part of the equation. However, there is that tempting urge to take advantage of whatever situations arise, which leads those with power to act for self-advantage. There are problem makers of minor and major proportions, but thankfully, there are also people who are huge contributors to the common good. Politicians exist at both ends of this spectrum, and the world desperately needs to have those, who are in positions of power over other people, be trustworthy contributors to the public good.

Keeping the proper perspective and not elevating oneself to a level of superiority can be difficult to achieve. Being the person in charge is fraught with temptations to promote one's self. Often, even those who are used to being the underling, when given the opportunity to be in an elevated position over other people, quickly forget what it felt like to be the disregarded underling.

Politics can deteriorate into underhandedness, or it can produce a united effort to work toward fair and even-handed solutions to problems. There is a mix, and often stalemates occur when there are power plays to stymie the opposition and create disorder instead of doing the responsible work of cooperatively solving problems, which urgently need attention. Years can go by with more muscles flexed than problems solved. Not infrequently, politicians behave more like football teams that are blocking and tackling instead of diplomatic negotiators whose main objective is to provide solutions to problems with fairness and justice in mind.

Not all politicians are going to agree on certain points, but the more willing they are to soften their agenda and thoughtfully consider what the opposition promotes, the more likely it will be that workable solutions will become apparent. Often politicians are like little children fighting over the possession of an object. The fight means more than the object itself. However, politicians are not willful children. They are supposed to be wise, diplomatic problem solvers and not self-serving conflict creators.

I recommend that every person who serves within governments take a pledge to serve selflessly and to the best of their ability to solve problems for the good of all. Then when stalemates occur, they should promote compromise, not of their ethics and morals, but of their strong-willed desire to dominate at all cost. Governments need diplomatic, ethical problem solvers. Governments do not need strong-willed big shots that primarily care about boosting their own egos and personal agendas.

It would be helpful if governments engaged more in a joint effort and compromise instead of separating into competing factions that are determined to gain power and hold onto it. Bringing in a more cooperative, problem-solving aspect to governing would encourage more compromising. Running governments is a job for fair-minded, conciliatory problem solvers who are devoted to improving on the systems already in place in an effort to serve all people better.

Conflict does not have to be a way of life. Dominance does not have to take precedence over cooperative action centered on the well-being of all people. There does not need to be a tug of war over who dictates or controls policy.

Working for the good of all is not that difficult to accomplish when this truly is the objective. Sure, there will be differing opinions and disagreements, but intelligent, flexible people are able to construct compromises that further the main objectives. Leaving personal egos out of negotiations and bringing along well-thought-out proposals and a desire to identify the most workable solutions will result in a joint action that is responsible and worthy of the trust placed in government.

I suggest that all negotiators sent to solve problems between two conflicting sides or multiple sides would do a better job if they incorporated three-dimensional perception skills. Three-dimensional perception keeps in mind the overall picture taking into account the impact on those represented in the negotiation as well as those not directly represented. Three-dimensional perception seeks to comprehend the complete state of affairs in order to bring justice and fairness across the board, not only to those represented but to all others as well.

When one develops three-dimensional perception, that person is ready to become an enlightened peacekeeper. Those that can perceive the nuances within conflicts and between opposing parties are more fully capable of playing a role in resolving them. With three-dimensional perception, opposing factions within governments would not be as likely to be at odds with each other as they often are now.

They would be more skilled at expanding their vision of possibilities to include those of the other sides and even beyond, to find the most constructive direction for the government to take. There are tremendous benefits to seeing all sides of issues and basing judgments and choices on an open-minded expansive assessment of the issue at hand. This approach is especially important within governing bodies whose judgments affect the well-being of great numbers of people who are depending on them to be fair and supportive.

Leaders within governments and corporations may have big egos with a puffed-up sense of self-worth, or they may be humbly working to perform their duties quietly and to the best of their ability. Many serve admirably and effectively. The best of the best consider themselves professionals who are determined to do the best job they can to fulfill their obligations.

These people should fill leadership positions within the government, business and society. Typically, they are best suited to further the general well-being of those they serve and society as a whole. Their character should be honorable, and their concern for others should not be a garment they put on to ensure their election.

Running for a position in government can be a deceitful position to undertake. First, there is the deceit that comes along with saying whatever is expedient to ensure the voters' approval, regardless of one's complete and true perspective on the issue. Then there is the deceit involved in casting adverse publicity against one's opponent to frighten voters away from giving that person their support.

Mudslinging against well-intentioned and qualified opponents often mars the business of running for political office. Deceit, deceit, deceit. Deceit is what is behind many successful election campaigns that do not yield the most qualified candidate as the winner.

Base the search for the most qualified candidate on an honest appraisal of the candidate's intentions and qualifications. Honesty should prevail instead of setting forth massive deceit and manipulation of what the opponent has said or done in order to inflame a negative reaction. Slurs, lies and manipulation often become apparent when power and control are at stake, and nothing will prevent this from continuing unless every person rises up to discredit any attempt to use these means to influence their vote.

I am aware of everyone's intentions. I am completely cognizant of deceitful allegations made against well-intentioned and honest political rivals. Anything gained through deceit is dishonest and does not carry the divine blessing that I give to those who are scrupulously honest.

The political arena has not been a field that promotes forthrightness and honesty, but it could be. A revolution would have to take place, and this is entirely possible. The revolution would begin with the voters.

Having the ability to cast a vote for exemplary leadership is a privilege and a responsibility. Those who do not have this option can take other steps, which involve standing up for the principles I have stated with their friends and neighbors and then stretching their influence beyond the local level. If enough people take this action, positive results will be forthcoming, and your world will change into a more reasonable and compassionate place to reside.

> Here are My instructions to voters that want to instill honor and truthfulness in the electoral process. **Do not let politicians manipulate you as if you were a puppet on a string.** Favor those running for office who stand up for what is good for all of humanity. Bringing prosperity to everyone should be the main goal, and you do not have to take from one group of people and give to another group to build prosperity.

Political problems are divisive because politicians typically pit one group against another and then try to get their group to align with them and against the other. There is a false presumption that not everyone can be well served. Politicians and voters need to understand that the best government is one that has the determination to address the problems and preferences of all their constituents evenhandedly. All people are entitled to the best that governments can provide for everyone under their jurisdiction.

I am in everyone. I have everyone as part of My composition and concern for the well-being of everyone as My nature. I want every one of My children to recognize that they are as important to Me as anyone else, and along with this, they must also recognize that everyone else is as important to Me as they are.

No one is preferred or favored. I am displeased when My children seek to elevate themselves over other people and cast some aside as not being worthwhile. Nothing hurts Me more than to feel what lies within those who have been pushed aside as being insignificant.

I shed tears for those shunned by their equals who may appear to be more favored because their lives may not be as difficult. I shed tears for humanity because many problems go unsolved and because very many people suffer while others prosper. I shed tears when dishonest and hurtful people take advantage of anyone but especially of honest, well-meaning people who are underprivileged and unable to have the benefits that others have during their lives. I shed tears for lost opportunities to help people, opportunities that pass by without a second thought as most people live their lives. I shed tears for the pain and sorrow that come about due to a lack of respect and humane treatment for all people.

I am encouraged by honesty, truthfulness and the will to do good. Universal will to do good would dull the pain and suffering of many, many people all over the world and give hope in place of despair. Every continent has cause for concern. In every corner of the Earth, there are people in need of assistance that they are not receiving. Every person on Earth has the ability to positively affect the lives of many people, and this is an important reason for My communication to all of you.

I want you to stop sitting on your hands and get to work. You may have problems of your own that feel insurmountable, but if you extend yourself to help another, you will be helping yourself as well. There is no better feeling than standing up for someone who needs support. Give them your support and then your friendship and you will be doing yourself a favor, as well.

People live on Earth in part to learn to value other people and to appreciate each other. I want everyone to become respectful of every other person and to enrich one's own life by putting your arms around others protectively and lovingly. This does not mean that I am asking you to hug every person you meet.

This does mean that I want you to honor and acknowledge the preciousness of every person. Then I want you to do whatever you can to spread joy and happiness, which may come from financial or emotional support. Never look down on any other person regardless of the life situation they have encountered.

Treat all with respect and concern for their well-being. In addition, never take advantage of another's desperate situation for self-gain. This type of activity is especially abhorrent to Me.

I have a gift for you when you are ready. When you reach a certain level of character development and turn your attention to finding Me within yourself, I give you My attention. I cause a stir within your conscience to guide you along the right path. I nudge you to take action that is upstanding, and you find yourself deeply attracted to My concepts that may sound foreign to you as you read about them now. I want each of you to become like Me, and you will, as you live lifetime after lifetime.

Each lifetime is precious for the character development that takes place. I delight in My children's advancement, and I am determined to quicken the evolutionary progress on Earth. However, not everyone is ready to embark upon a path that calls for loving and accepting all other people.

The urge to blame, criticize and punish runs deep within the human psyche, as does the urge to value some people as being more worthwhile than others. You may say that these traits express human nature, and they do, but that does not mean that individuals cannot improve themselves. Everyone is able to refine himself or herself when they are willing to put forth the effort. People can educate themselves out of acting instinctively instead of compassionately and humanely.

People in general recoil at the cruelty displayed around the world. The level of savagery in some places escalates to horrific levels as innocents, including precious children, take the brunt of violence imposed upon them by malcontents' objective to harm and destroy other people. Human beings are creative, but in too many instances, their innovations have to do with ways to create havoc in the lives of others.

It does not take an intellectually superior person to understand that the world is becoming a more dangerous place to live, and this is due to the outrageously destructive way certain people feel and act towards others.

> Some people pray to Me to make things on Earth better, but this is the responsibility of each and every person to bring about by reforming themselves. I am not going to hold up an untenable situation on Earth so people can continue their misguided ways.

I am giving you basic information that is required to forestall impending disastrous happenings on Earth. It is up to all of you to do what you can by addressing your personal areas of deficiency and overcoming them as effectively as you can.

Individuals in leadership positions and politicians can play a powerful role in instituting needed improvements, but a certain number of them will have to do a wholesale reorganization of how they operate to create an example for the rest of the population of how to act responsibly and cooperatively for the good of all.

Doing this will provide a big impetus to those under their jurisdiction to follow suit. Those governing officials who catch on and take significant steps in this direction will experience unusual effectiveness and respect. Those officials who do not follow this path are likely to lose respect and relevance.

Only minimal improvement will occur if people take these steps half-heartedly and without significant follow-through. Although any improvement will be positive, minimal improvement is not good enough. Your world cannot wait any longer for people to wise up that the way they typically do things is not working very well, and if collective, positive action is not taken right away, it will be too late to avert even greater dissolution of decency and respect for all people.

I urge every person to embrace the education that I am presenting to you. Appoint yourself as My representative, exhibiting My characteristics in your daily life. There is no better, more effective way to guarantee a life worth living for the generations to come who will model their behavior after what they see around them as they grow into adulthood.

Now is the time to reinvent today's world, making it a peaceful, safe and satisfying place for all people. Begin immediately. Do not think about waiting until tomorrow. Wrap your mind around the principles I stated in these first three chapters. Then perform your self-analysis and begin the assignment of modifying your perceptions and behaviors to match Mine.

I have no doubt that what I am asking you to do is achievable. Everyone who participates will benefit by experiencing the good feelings that automatically develop within him or her, as they successfully incorporate more ethical and considerate behavior. This happens to all who raise their standards of behavior to match Mine. Reflect My morals and ethics and then experience the dramatically comforting changes that take place in one's sense of well-being. My desire for all My children is to exist in a state of joyousness and to radiate love and compassion to all.

CHAPTER FOUR

ACCURATE SELF-KNOWLEDGE

———

What pleases you most when you look over your life thus far? What gives you the most satisfaction? It may surprise you to know that rising to a high level of worldly success is not the greatest achievement a person can attain.

Do not misunderstand Me. If you rise to a heightened level of worldly success, I am happy for you, for your enjoyment and sense of accomplishment. However, I am far more impressed when a person responds that they are pleased that they treated themselves and their bodies respectfully and regarded other people considerately.

Life's activities have an ebb and flow about them. There are times when things go well, and you feel that you are making forward progress. Life is satisfying. Then there are times that require fierce determination to get through. Outwardly, something may or may not have changed, but inwardly one feels stress and dissatisfaction with how life is going in some area or another.

When these challenging times set in, realize that your inner self is urging you to raise your behavior to a more evolved level than you have previously attained. Do not give in to misery, self-loathing, drugs or alcohol. Go inward and place your attention on finding your personal weaknesses, such as character deficiencies or behavioral deficits. Put this fertile time to good use by culling out habitual traits, thoughts or behaviors that are not supporting your further progress as an evolving human being. Your opportunity to make the most progress in overcoming your personal deficiencies is during these uncomfortable down times.

Whether or not you maximize the opportunities for inner growth during these down periods, in time, these stressing periods will pass, and you will feel like your old self again. You will be active and find your life satisfying unless you turned to drugs or alcohol during the down period. If that is the case, you have helped yourself to another set of problems to deal with. I am dismayed when people turn to drugs, alcohol, sexual promiscuity and other dishonorable behavior. It takes lifetimes of many years for people to evolve their behavioral patterns, and in a matter of a few years of undisciplined conduct, they may lose much of the progress they previously made.

Although it seems like you start over with every lifetime, each lifetime piggybacks onto the last lifetime. Your goal is to make evolutionary progress during each life you live. Do not set yourself back because you lose focus on your responsibility to yourself to become the best person that you can be. You are important to Me, each and every one of you, and I want you to be important to yourself. Do not do anything that will bring you sadness and regret down the road.

If you wonder why you might be more vulnerable than other people seem to be in entangling yourself in drugs, alcohol or other character weakening behaviors, consider that you might be more sensitive to life's disappointments. Over sensitivity makes one feel more pain and disappointment than other people who may undergo the same experience but are not as sensitive. On the positive side, extremely sensitive people are more likely to empathize with those who are downtrodden.

Sensitive people's hearts have an expanded capacity to reach out to others with tenderness and caring. If you need to be consoled, go to a sensitive, tenderhearted person to hold your hand. You will feel better, and so will they as they give you their support.

Now I will tell you something that might surprise you. Almost all of you have a tendency to be hard on yourself. Tough judgment can supersede forgiving tenderness when you become aware of personal shortcomings or your negative impact on other people. Unfortunately, after delivering a negative impact, few people retain their discomfort with themselves, and most people dismiss it from their minds as soon as they can.

Ignoring one's shortcomings or offenses is never going to help you to eliminate them from your catalog of behaviors. Nearly everyone walks around with whitewash and a delete button. They both come in handy to escape taking responsibility for what one does or says that is underhanded.

In a flash, one deletes or covers over with whitewash, something they said or did that was dishonest or truly uncivilized. Then they walk away from an opportunity to come clean with themselves. Would it not be more advantageous for everyone to own up to his or her offenses, faults and shortcomings?

There is something in the human psyche that cringes when one has no other option than to acknowledge a defective characteristic within them self. The urge to deny the obvious trait or action is a self-protective mechanism calculated to keep one's ego intact. The ego exists to give one inner strength and not to prop up a person's inner self-concepts. I will tell you what does make you feel worthwhile. Be authentic with yourself.

Authenticity comes from deep within oneself. It rises up within a person when that person is not ashamed of their imperfections even as they are striving to eliminate them. They have no urge to appear better than any other person as they maintain calm detachment from life's volatility. They remain grounded within their own nature, having little need for attention, the spotlight or boasting. In their deeply satisfied state, they nurture themselves from within.

The greatest life satisfaction comes from two sources: having a positive impact on other people, especially those in need of outside support, and from shedding the insecurity that most people inherently have within themselves. Realize that the more flashy and attention-seeking you are, the more difficult it will be to bring forth your authentic self, unobstructed by a need to prove your worthwhileness to the world. The high road in life is taking the adventure within oneself to discover the faultless integrity hidden deep inside every human being.

Life is an adventure filled with thrills, delights, hardships and confusion. I do not want any of you to pass from this life without your fair share of life's ups and downs and turnarounds. It is the turnarounds that most delight Me.

There are people who are born into distressing circumstances who rise up through force of will and sheer determination to lead exemplary lives. I do not mind if you create a lot of drama, highs and lows during your lifetime. I want you to use those twists and turns to become cognizant of who you really are before you earn your ticket home to enjoy a rest between lifetimes.

When I see various people, I notice what truly is significant. What shines forth to My vision is their inner beauty honed by acts of honesty, compassion and kindness. I particularly notice how invested they are in upholding high moral and ethical standards and if they even consider their morals and ethics. A great number of people do not focus on much other than their desires of the moment.

Desire is the main motivating factor and generally is what propels people to do what they decide to do. Desires fall into two basic categories: the desire to express oneself and the desire to get ahead. Some people have a strong inner urge to be number one, the person at the top of the ladder. The urge to be number one is a challenging urge to manage, for the urge itself invites an oversized ego along with a skewed code of ethics.

Most people rise to positions of authority based on their qualifications, aptitudes and past accomplishments. Others, who may or may not have the same history of achievement, may strive mightily to obtain power and glamor expected to accompany being in the top position. Those who hunger for status and power are more likely to abandon their code of ethics in order to get what they want. My point in bringing attention to this subject is to emphasize that all people have a strong obligation to act from a moral and ethical base of conduct at all times and under all circumstances.

I am waiting for the day when all My children love each other as much as I love them. If people can love and respect their friends and their family members, they have what it takes to hold everyone else in high regard as well. Millions of people everywhere hold back from genuinely reaching out to others even though they are open-minded, loving people. Old habits may keep some people from going forward to extend themselves with cordiality to people who they do not know or people who seem different than they are.

I propose that warm-hearted people begin a movement to extend kindness, courtesy and congeniality as a general plan for their lives. I would like them to focus specifically on including people who do not share their same background. Everyone needs to break down the invisible barriers that needlessly separate My children from acknowledging each other and becoming close to one another.

Most of the people on Earth are capable of eradicating their prejudices. Typically, people hang onto prejudices because they are a familiar habit to which they do not give much thought, and it does not help when their peers share the same prejudices. Most prejudices are hand-downs from previous generations, mindlessly accepted by the new generations that come along. Accepting what someone else thinks or believes does not make sense unless it passes one's own litmus test.

I admonish you not to hold prejudice against any person. Prejudice is a vile poison, which prevents willing acceptance of the value of every person. If every person came to interact with other people without knowing their background or anything about them, and two of them sat down and talked to each other, they would not only have a lot in common, but they would grow to like each other. In most cases, this is exactly what would happen. People's stale prejudices prevent automatic acceptance of other people.

Some people are prejudiced against themselves. They hold ill perceptions about themselves and allow these to interfere with their personal well-being. They do not reach out to others with a clear mind and open heart because they do not feel comfortable just being themselves.

I do not hold back from accepting and loving every person, and I do not want anyone to hold back from extending themselves to others because of low self-esteem. Even famous and successful people can run into this detrimental problem, which can only be overcome by the person valuing themself. People's yardsticks differ and may be the problem when one falls short in their self-concepts.

People that compare themselves to people who are dazzling others with their talents or personalities are looking for trouble. I do not want people to compare themselves with other people. I am most interested in how people express themselves uniquely. You see, I have created no one else exactly like you, and I am not interested in having you mimic any other person. I want you to express yourself creatively and individually. Therein lies the satisfaction in life.

Each person has My creative impulse within them, waiting to manifest and being different from anyone else's. Always value yourself as being the equal of other people, and do not hold back your self-expression because you do not feel that you are up to other people's standards. Authenticity is part of what makes people appealing. Everyone enjoys being with someone that dares to be completely comfortable in their own skin. It is very refreshing to hear another person reveal one of their shortcomings without flinching, and it is most uncomfortable to attempt to hide one's own shortcomings.

> Accepting oneself is one of life's challenges that lands in everyone's lap to deal with, and each will know that they have succeeded when they feel comfortable being with people who seem to be very personable and successful, without feeling inferior.

Valuing oneself may not be easy. People turn to various means to gain feelings of self-worth, creating accomplishments being one of them. One would think that a long list of accomplishments automatically generates self-esteem, yet often this is not what occurs. Even those of high achievement may not accept themselves as being inherently worthwhile. The motivation for their effort to achieve may be to prove to themselves and the exterior world that they are a worthwhile person.

People who value themselves do not have to prove their value to anyone else. They may be and often are high achievers, but their feelings of self-worth are not dependent upon their outward success. Outward success may reinforce their positive self-concepts but does not create them.

I instill positive self-concepts within everyone as part of their heritage. If it were not for the upsetting atmosphere that can occur within households or demeaning school experiences, more children would develop higher self-esteem and be more likely to mature into adults who value themselves. I give all people admirable qualities and attributes that they can use as a base to build genuine self-esteem, which will flourish unless their self-esteem diminishes because of detrimental happenings around them.

Nearly everyone's life has intrusions that are undermining and may affect one's self-esteem. People who are not cognizant of the harmful impact of their behavior or, if they are aware, they do not care, initiate negative impacts upon others. When this occurs, people whose self-esteem is already wobbly and children are most deeply affected.

I recommend that every person take an inventory of their actions, moods and behaviors to detect any that may be putting a burden upon a child or anyone else, which could lead that person to lose self-esteem. If you are an adult, picture yourself as a child having to listen to degrading speech or arguing, and think about how this would affect your feeling of safety and security. Then stop yourself if you begin to go down that road. We could perform various exercises to bring home the point I am making, but it should not be necessary. **If you are a person that disrupts another person's well-being through negligence, ignorance or deliberate action, you are ultimately responsible**

for the negative effect that your behavior has upon the other person.

Do not be someone who devalues other people. Have a heart and treat every person as you would want him or her to treat you. Respect others and earn their respect in return. You will enjoy the feelings of self-worth that this will give you. My plan for the human race is for everyone everywhere to love, respect and care about everyone else.

My plan also entails accurately evaluating oneself. Too many people do not give themselves enough credit for their inherent quiet goodness. They glow inside with My presence. This is their natural way to be, and they may not recognize what a blessing they are. If more people were as they are, your world's discord and resentment would tone down. Getting along with other people would be more enjoyable and less of a challenge than it often is.

Those who do not perceive themselves accurately are typically the ones who are more likely to stir up trouble and point the finger of blame at another person. As a result, resentment simmers and the instigator has no awareness of their culpability. They may go on resenting the person who was their target, firmly believing that the innocent person was the one who created the discord. Inaccurate self-knowledge tends to throw relationships off-kilter and may sink them altogether.

Taking a realistic look at oneself when there is discord with another is as difficult as trying to swallow a pillow. If people knew how many times they were mistaken when they held another person accountable for what they themselves brought about, they would be mortified. Stubbornness and defensiveness are twin causes of unresolved discord between people. How refreshing it would be if the knee-jerk reaction to conflict were to block the instinct to protect one's self from culpability and then perform an honest self-appraisal. When people get up enough courage and moral fiber to shoulder responsibility for what they themselves bring about, simmering resentments, animosity and prolonged inner upheaval will not appear with the same regularity that they typically do.

Part of My reason for speaking out now is to awaken My precious children to what they themselves create that causes problems for themselves and other people too. Their self-shielding instincts lead them to blame other people for what they are responsible for instigating. More often than not, people interpret whatever disruption occurs as being the result of someone else behaving poorly instead of himself or herself. I am committed to awakening My children everywhere to the importance of knowing themselves accurately and taking full responsibility for what they create.

Everyone's lives are intermingled with the lives of untold numbers of other people, and predictably, very few understand their impact on others. At times discord erupts even within sound relationships and puts a strain on compatibility. Within seconds, a compatible relationship can fracture, sending both parties into defensiveness.

Do not be too quick to hold the other party fully responsible for creating the problems. Even if they are, your swift rush to judgment may discourage them from honestly assessing themselves. They are more likely to go straight into thoughts of retaliation. Whatever you do, do not produce an extension of the conflict. The fault may lie squarely on the shoulders of one person, but it is going to take both parties to forge an understanding to end the conflict.

Ending a conflict may take no more than shutting one's mouth and listening to the other person rant and rave about wrongs inflicted upon them. Some people need to vent their steam, and when they do, their emotions go back into balance. They get themselves out of the stew they were in by disgorging their fury. It takes enormous self-control to listen quietly while being accused of offensive behavior when you do not agree with the other person's assessment of the situation. However, many times this is your best option.

Most interpersonal conflicts will resolve by allowing the accuser to vent without adding to the discord by taking defensive action that would only serve to add more flames to the fire. Then when rationality returns, the situation will calm and, with both sides becoming more objective and sensible, mutually agreeable resolutions are more likely to become apparent. Other interpersonal conflicts are not as easily resolved, and this is when both parties see things their way and have no interest in finding a middle ground. It is their way or the highway, and often these situations result in fractured relationships that do not become reconciled. Individuals are not the only ones that box themselves into a corner with ultimatums such as these.

Anyone with the upper hand in organizations can make this demand and push through decisions that may not be sound or ethical. When one holds the seat of power and does not pay adequate attention to advisors who are clear thinking and rational, the organization may not advance in the best direction. People need to confer with each other when disagreements arise and when solutions to conflicts or other problems are required. The *my way or the highway* approach is for hot heads who are more involved with their power urge than in crafting lasting and fair solutions to conflicts and other problems.

If you could see the world as I do, your heart would ache, as Mine does, over the degree of conflict that weaves throughout societies. Conflict seems to be a part of human nature. I invite everyone to examine his or her own life and the lives of others with whom they are familiar to gain sharper awareness of the degree of conflict that exists within daily life.

Most interpersonal conflicts occur when people cannot stop thinking about a happening that they interpret as being an assault against them by another party. They think about the alleged wrongdoing, usually exaggerating the circumstances in their mind, until they feel justified in taking action against whomever they hold responsible for their discomfort. Do not allow what other people say or do to over-heat you and, if you feel that you are being mistreated, choose a time when you are calm and rational to talk to that person.

Begin the conversation by communicating your concerns but as you speak, monitor yourself to be sure you are speaking truthfully and not exaggerating. Monitor your emotions and keep them level. Even if you follow these instructions, your success will depend on the other person's receptivity.

One of the biggest challenges a person can have is for someone to confront them and accuse them of wrongdoing. Usually, this will set off one's internal alarm system, and they prepare to defend themselves. It requires self-control and maturity to listen to accusations that seem out of balance or totally trumped up and not lose one's self-control, but this is the key to decompressing the situation. Once the accuser has laid out their case and not run into a defensive comeback, they usually back off and calm down. Many times this is all that it takes for someone who has been fuming with discontent to disengage from the urge to stay in it.

Even when it seems that the discontented person has little or no grounds to be upset, it is of utmost importance to assume that they do and review the accusations with an eye to discovering the merit in their perception. Do not shirk from being completely honest with yourself. Something is amiss when these conflicts arise, and it may be that one side or the other may be the sole cause, but more often than not, each bears some responsibility.

Most of these instances of discord pass by and are forgotten, especially when both parties are honest with each other and with themselves, and there is no emotional investment in clinging to hurt feelings.

Relationships are challenging, especially when emotions rule. One's emotional base must be stable to get along with other people. Runaway emotions empower people to do and say things, which lead to conflict. Then they tend to blame the other person. Blow-ups caused by a person without emotional stability can lead to confusion as to who is responsible for the problem that arises, in part because they typically see themselves as blameless. Interpersonal relationships are much smoother between people who do their best to remain calm and slow to react to perceived offenses.

Human nature is varied. Some people are mild-mannered and tend to be agreeable. They are often flexible and tend to fit in well with others. Some are entertaining attention-seekers who may delight or upset other people. Usually, these people feel empowered when the spotlight is shining on them, and they either entertain or produce conflict, enjoying every minute of it.

You may enjoy them, or you may dislike them, but one thing is certain – you notice them. People have different ego needs, which are apparent by how they present themselves. I incorporated variety into the human race, and I treasure everyone's distinctive self-presentation.

I wish everyone appreciated the endless variety of people's personalities, traits and characteristics as I do. On Earth, people tend to gravitate to their look-alikes. They tend to huddle together with people who reflect themselves in many ways. Coming from the same socio-economic or ethnic group, the same religious persuasion or sharing strong convictions, political or otherwise, brings people together with a thread of commonality. This may be comfortable, but it may induce a sectioning off from people who would bring the richness of expanded perceptions and experiences.

It would delight Me if everyone in the world changed places with another person to see what the other person's life is like and to help them in any way that they could. This would delight Me tremendously, for then you would be acting as if I were there in person. You would be doing for each other what I do for you. I am with you every day as you live your life. You probably do not know that I am experiencing your daily life and that I am available to assist you.

The closer you draw to Me, the more I will make My presence known to you. I am a readily available resource. I cannot overemphasize My willingness to become a conscious, active part of your life. If you think this is an impossibility, you are mistaken. I am giving you this information to set the stage for a closer relationship between us.

Everyone on Earth is on a path of personal development that will lead to a conscious realization that they are a part of Me and that everyone else is a part of Me, as well. This is a huge leap forward from the common illusion that every person is separate. Nothing exists outside of Myself. All that you see around you is Me in My many different forms.

Your consciousness springs from what you perceive as an individual, whereas I enjoy the total experience of all creation simultaneously. Your vision is not as broad as Mine, but if it were, you would have the same perceptions and attitudes that I do.

On Earth, misunderstanding is common. No one sees himself or herself as being more than they appear to be when in reality, each person is an independent component of the entirety of My being. Grasping that each person is a part of the Divine Presence is the light that needs illumination in everyone's mind.

I understand that this concept will surprise many people, and with good reason, for most people do not present themselves as being part of divinity. People judge themselves and other people by what they do, how they appear and what they believe. Using these criteria alone is not a failsafe way to determine their linage.

I am waiting for every person to come to the realization that they are divine offspring and that all other people are as well. No one is less than another in My eyes, and sooner or later, every person's perspective will match Mine. The world in which you live does not properly appreciate the value of other people or the value of each person's self, for that matter. What is obvious to Me escapes awareness within the physical world.

> Intrinsic goodness is within every person. The spark of divinity that is implanted within all creation resides within every human being regardless of who they are or what they do.

Most people have no idea of the goodness that lies within them because tarnishing attitudes and behaviors obscure their goodness. People judge by what they see and not by what remains hidden from view. I, on the other hand, have full knowledge of the goodness covered over, waiting to be uncovered within people everywhere. Even those who appear to be on the right track of becoming gracious, ethical and caring have no idea of their depths of empathy and ability to assist others that they have yet to bring forth. Your world is in great need of everyone reaching for their intrinsic goodness, pulling it out, and making it the foundation of their existence.

I challenge you to go out of your way to interact with people who you may have been overlooking as you go about your daily routines. Ignite the world with genuine caring for one another and spread the caring broadly. Do not put restrictions on who you hold as being significant or important. Kindly make allowances for those who have yet to become aware of the preciousness of all people, even as you begin to resonate with tender feelings toward all of humanity. Take on My view of the preciousness of everyone and become My surrogate to demonstrate how I am.

This is what I advise. Consider every person on Earth as a member of one's precious family. Strive to promote a unified sense of positive relationship with all countries and within each country a unified sense of the importance of every person. This means working together with the intention of safeguarding the well-being of all people and holding no tolerance for any form of targeting or destructive action imposed on any people.

Human beings need to become each other's champions and protectors. Hold high standards of valuing all other people and step forward to thwart injustice and cruelty.

When you lift someone who needs your assistance, when you step forward to shield another from pain or hardship, when you nurture someone who needs comforting, you are acting from your god-ness within. Feel My presence come forward within you at these times especially and delight with Me at the positive impact we are manifesting together.

CHAPTER FIVE

GRACIOUSNESS AND COMPROMISE

———

I especially value people who are gracious and skilled in the art of compromise. Learning to compromise builds character and leads to better solutions, which proves the old adage that two heads are better than one. By combining what is important to differing sides of an issue into the formation of solutions, the process brings about a more wholesome resolution. Less discord between factions, along with more respectful paying attention to other people's needs and desires, can provide the cement that holds communities together.

By mentally putting oneself in the place of the other party and thoughtfully considering what they want from their perspective, overall perception expands, providing a platform from which more enlightened solutions will spring forth. Some giving up by one party can influence the other party to be more agreeable and may avoid needless conflict that occurs when one party is trying to get everything they want and are unwilling to concede anything to the other. Often two parties who are in disagreement draw a curtain between them.

This curtain is invisible but can be as strong as steel. Each side repels the other as if they were a skunk. This is how human beings remain conflict-bound and disgusted with the erroneously perceived perpetrator of the problem. There is no resolution that will satisfy both parties when it is an *either/or* situation. This is what causes stalemates to occur.

If there is any chance for people to get along with each other when they do not see eye to eye, it can only come about through compromise. Being willing to compromise is not a sign of weakness, as many would hold. Compromise leads to opposing parties building respect between them. Compromise brings about a sharing of the marbles instead of one person carrying all the marbles in their pocket. Only when the issue of contention involves the safety and security of people should there be no give and take. There is an absolute divine law that people's lives are to be respected and never squandered.

Every person is a candidate for becoming a warm, gracious individual who is able to express genuine caring for all other people. You may question if what I have just said is indeed true. There are certain prerequisites that need to be in place for this to happen.

First, the flame of genuine caring for all other people must ignite within one's heart and mind. Often the mind gets in the way of one's impulse to act from their heart. If people's minds did not route through their past conditioning of how to view certain other people, the heart's instinct to act graciously toward others would win out.

Many excellent negotiators who are gracious become highly respected masters of the art of compromise. Graciousness conveys caring about the other party, truly caring and not just putting up a front. Truly caring for other people is a most desirable quality to have, for it makes one's self an instrument of compatibility.

In difficult situations, graciousness and congeniality are typically in short supply. Often tempers flare, and a tug of war begins as each party maneuvers to get their own way. Two dogs fighting over a bone are often as compatible as two people on opposite sides of a contentious issue who will not calm down and thoughtfully listen to the different point of view.

Keep in mind that personal warmth melts cold resistance and creates compatibility. The warmth that people reserve for their loved ones may also extend to the other people with whom one associates. If everyone on Earth decided to treat everyone else as someone who was beloved to them, there would be smiles all around.

There is no reason to devalue other people, their needs or opinions. All are My beloved children, and I am loving them every minute of every day. I want My children to hold each other close and to love each other as I love them.

Gracious people tend to attune to other people's feelings. They extend themselves to others with congeniality and openness that invites closeness. Everyone would prefer a genuinely gracious interaction rather than those that are perfunctory. Graciousness builds respectful relationships, which bring harmony and sharing instead of the closed door of arrogance.

Taking a genuine interest in other people invites respect and consideration in return. With gracious interactions, trust builds along with compatibility and willingness to compromise in order to satisfy the concerns of all sides. The lost art of being gracious even to one's adversaries is of utmost importance to develop.

Listening with an open mind is another of life's most important skills to incorporate within oneself. Often people's minds are like a team of runaway horses going in a strongly defined direction and creating havoc along the way. I would like to present every person with an automatic pause button that they could use to stop their knee-jerk opposition to what other people say, especially when they believe the other person is wrong. It is almost impossible to consider another person's point of view in an unbiased manner if you already assumed the other person is wrong.

Before crossing a busy street, it is important to stop, look and listen. I urge you to do the same when you receive someone else's opinion, which conflicts with your own. Look at them thoughtfully, giving them your full attention, and listen with an open mind to what they have to say. Then pause to evaluate their reasoning. Control the need to push your own point of view until you have fully considered the other person's position.

Too often, people think they have a better grasp of an issue than another who holds a differing opinion without having investigated the reasoning behind the other person's perceptions.

Depending upon one's background and personal history, individuals are more likely to cling to certain viewpoints and positions. Others with different backgrounds and life experiences often tend to hold differing positions on the same issue. It would benefit both parties to strive to understand the reasoning behind their different perspectives by putting themselves in the shoes of the opposing party. I am talking about letting go of one's position and fully jumping into the perspective of the other party to understand their reasoning.

The logical next step is to rethink the issue and look for ways to blend solutions that support both sides, which usually requires compromise. Teamwork accomplishes more than a tug of war. Teamwork creates a companionable atmosphere where everyone is pulling in the direction of implementing the best solution for the issue at hand.

This goes for members of a family who are trying to decide where to go on vacation as well as within the walls of government where the stakes are much higher. Too often, egos dominate, and the powerful enforce what may be inferior propositions over better proposals, which are not fully considered. Within all levels of society, the dominant personalities, and especially the hot heads, need to become thoughtful listeners to what people who do not agree with them have to say.

Powerful people often feel that they deserve to dictate policy. Decisions generated from a seat of power often tend to be self-serving and ignorant of the needs of those who do not have a voice in that conversation. The world is full of powerful people who go elbow to elbow to get their way over wise council that recommends otherwise. Powerful or not, the best way to determine policy is to listen thoughtfully to all sides of an issue and avoid the impulse to only factor in personal advantages.

Representing a government or an organization puts oneself in an elevated position of responsibility, which typically requires astute problem-solving and management skills.

> Another rarely stated requirement that I would put at the top of the list is high morality. High morality is rarely a consideration but should be included as another prerequisite for a high-level position.

At times, morally wrong and sometimes very reprehensible decisions come from the higher levels of an organization. When one does not stand up for taking the moral high road and instead abandons their moral compass, I am saddened. Even though one's allegiance is to the institution they represent, there is a duty to protect the well-being of the people affected by those decisions.

One cannot disown responsibility for what they are instrumental in bringing about even though they may not feel that they have a choice. I am instructing those who are making decisions, including those who are enforcing the instructions of the higher-ups, to use humanitarian considerations and to speak up when violations occur. Do not remain silent. Remaining silent in these situations is tantamount to having made the initial decision oneself.

The minions of powerful people who assign others the dirty work have carried out crimes against humanity. Carrying out one's assignment when it is damaging to other people and ignoring the ethical and moral issues involved is like eating whatever is put in front of you even when it is rotten. My higher authority demands fair treatment for all people under all circumstances. When a person holds the well-being of other people in their hands, they should be acting as I would act. I would never impose any form of damage to a person's well-being.

Understand that there is a punitive instinct within some people, and with this punitive instinct comes a desire to impose it. Combine this punitive instinct with righteous indignation, and the formula for attacking innocent people appears. With punitive righteousness, one is likely to bring loathsome hurtful actions onto those they decide to target.

I am sickened by the harm done to My precious children in the name of God. Using one's unenlightened self to determine My preferences is not acceptable to Me. I am not as many people have assumed that I am. If you want to please Me, embrace My other children and safeguard them. Carry My love in your heart and never act to deliberately injure any other person.

Your world needs amicable interactions between all people, and I would especially champion cordial interactions with people who are decidedly different from each other. Most people gravitate to those who are similar to themselves in background and beliefs. This does not expand points of view or angles of perception.

It is more broadening to become acquainted with people who have different backgrounds and beliefs. Most people would be surprised at how much they have in common with people of different backgrounds and how easily they can relate. With the separating distinctions of *them* and *us* removed, the world can be as I intended it to be: a place to become acquainted with people who do not look like oneself in the mirror.

Respect grows when people know each other authentically and not from stereotypical imaginings. Stereotypical definitions of what other people are like is the same as looking at the outside to know what is inside of a person. Exterior appearances do not accurately convey that which lies within. Consider a kiwi fruit that does not look appetizing from its exterior appearance, but if one passes it up because of its appearance, they will miss tasting a delicious treat. I would like all My children to become open to knowing and interacting with people who are very different than themselves and to become educated in the many different forms of beauty and attractiveness that are instilled within the human race.

> Graciousness is what I extend to all of you by loving you unconditionally, and this is what I desire for you to do for each other as well. Graciously accepting all other people destroys underhandedness and produces untold benefits that your world desperately needs.

One could hardly call the world in which you live a lovingly considerate place to be, although it has the potential to become exactly that, but it will take unified commitment and effort on the part of every individual to achieve this worthy goal in their own life. As people revise their previously set behavior to include an automatic sending forth of loving respect to all people, without picking and choosing who one thinks is deserving, your world will become a more serene and friendlier place to live.

In a world where every person can count on being respected, conflicts are rare. Sure, people will still disagree about this and that, but there is common adherence to a higher code of ethics that prevails over one's emotional discontent. You can create this benign formula even on Earth, but it will take self-control uniformly practiced within each individual. Hotheads lead to unwise actions that create conflict. Egos and pride must take a back seat to the objective of creating a benign world in which to live.

Most people would like to reside in a peaceful, pleasant atmosphere and be able to count on other people to come to their aid when they need assistance. Many people would be delighted to extend a helping hand to someone who had a legitimate need, especially when they know them. We see this when neighbors help each other. Take into consideration a family with not enough food who needs support but whose neighbors are unable to help because they are no better off.

Impoverished people who desperately need assistance are typically isolated from the well-to-do who seem to live in a different world entirely. Impoverished people need sponsors and helping hands to pull them up and give them a chance in life.

I am instructing everyone to share the commitment of helping other people, especially those who are most in need of compassionate support. Search out those with great need, including those who may be far from where you are and, if you cannot help them directly, work through an established organization with pristine credentials.

I am most displeased when charities pay out much less than the sum donated and keep the rest for their organization. Even more appalling is the siphoning off or outright stealing of aid intended for needy people depriving them of much-needed sustenance. When giving to those in need, do your best to choose the right source of delivery so your gift of caring will reach its intended destination.

Only those who know Me well can understand My insistence on equal treatment for all people. Only those who know Me well share My deep feelings of love and respect for all people, regardless of their performance thus far. I am confident that each of you will come to understand Me better as you develop My qualities within yourself. The way that I am becomes the natural way for people to be as they progress through the process of refining their attributes and behaviors. No one starts from too low of a position to accomplish this.

Although mistaken thinking and plenty of misjudgments abound, deep down inside, everyone is a replica of Myself that is obscured and covered over with confusion. The confusion is difficult to sort out without explanation and instruction. I do not fault anyone for being confused. By looking at the world in which you live and taking your cues from what you see around you, it is almost impossible to model yourself after the way I am.

A replica of Myself does not come to the forefront in typical interactions between people. A replica of Myself is not evident in the turmoil and the disgraceful attitudes and actions of unenlightened people. I am within your heart and your conscience. When people have pure hearts and highly developed consciences, My presence within them shows.

I am in all the noble qualities that people exhibit and in those splendid qualities, which are not readily apparent to others. I take every opportunity to expand My presence into a recognizable vibration of god-ness within those who deliberately take on My characteristics. I invite everyone to follow My lead and become as I am.

I am apparent in the negotiators that are fair-minded. I am apparent in the people who do charitable work with a smile on their faces. I am apparent within people who sacrifice their well-being to aid another person.

I am apparent in the warm-hearted caretakers of children, and I am apparent in Mom and Pop, who do their best to raise their children with love, respect and a dedication to being fair-minded and supportive of them. I am apparent in the volunteers that appear during times of tragedy to rescue those who are in desperate need. I appear openly in many human forms when people are acting with love and compassion and putting other people's well-being at the forefront of their concern.

In other words, I am where people act to aid others with pure hearts and with the highest intentions to benefit them with no thought of recouping a reward for themselves.

Notice how this contrasts with those who flex their muscles and stuff their pocketbooks. Who do you think are closer to Me: those who give of themselves willingly to help another person or those who grab for themselves all they can get? Those who act ruthlessly or those who have a strict personal code of conduct? I am in everyone, but My presence is openly expressed only in those who do their best to live by My principles of loving all other people and lending a helping hand without regard to being rewarded.

Everyone has the potential to bring out My presence within them more noticeably than they have before. I am explaining what it takes to begin to experience My presence from the beginner level to the more advanced levels. Everyone can start where he or she currently is and progress upward from that point. There is no race except the race to be rewarded with definite confirmation that I am within you and acting through you to embrace My other children, especially in times of hardship.

Acting with the intention in your mind to be completely honest and generous of spirit and reaching out to your sisters and brothers around the world with loving acceptance will put you on the fast track to building My presence strongly within you.

You may wonder what My presence feels like. First, there is the light tingling within your body that you are likely to dismiss as being in your imagination. Following this is the urge to reform yourself and to take the right, ethical path at all times. You will find yourself questioning your intentions and your performance to see if you were acting from a high base of integrity. After a while, you will know yourself better than before, and you will catch yourself when you are letting your standards slip.

This is a lengthy yet rewarding process, especially when signs appear that wondrous transformation is seeding within your entire being. Your attitudes will improve not because you are forcing them to but because the divine flow has been established within you and is starting to show. You may not be the first person to notice.

The people around you may catch on before you do because they will be enjoying the subtle changes within your self-expression. You will hear yourself saying uncharacteristically wise things that will surprise you. Life will smooth out for you, and even though challenges remain, they will not toss you around as they used to.

If a person running for an elective position had My presence firmly anchored within them, they would receive nearly all the votes because they would appeal to everyone. They would clearly be the best choice for the position as they radiated wisdom and concern for the well-being of everyone. That they were scrupulously honest would be readily apparent, and their personal magnetism would be palpable. Can you imagine how this would feel to have these qualities starting to appear within you?

There is every reason for people everywhere to embrace what I am teaching. I am defining how to make your life experience become extraordinarily satisfying.

The hardest part is getting started because switching over from being self-centered, judgmental and stuck in bad habits to becoming self-aware and self-correcting takes a lot of determination and constant effort.

Consider uprooting a plant that is growing in dry, rocky soil and then replanting it in a soil rich in nutrients with ample rainfall. At first, that plant is going to go through a very uncomfortable state after you uproot it. It will have lost its firm foundation and be dangling without the support that it used to have. This uncomfortable time is what people go through when they realize they have to remove what they considered their firm footing in order for them to evolve. It can be disorienting to have to give up how they previously constructed themselves even though most would freely admit that they are not a poster child for having all the right qualities and values.

Upgrading oneself from one's current level of self-development is a daunting task. When you begin, do not expect this endeavor to be easy. Work steadily and celebrate every success that you have. Expect a lengthy adjustment period, which requires watchfulness, self-control and inner reorganization of values and behaviors. Over time, the payoff will be joyous as you make progress along this path of sweeping out those traits and behaviors that are not worth holding onto.

It is senseless to continue along the path of discord and incompatibility that is prevalent around the world. I do not want My precious children to keep living in a fog of confusion and behave in ways that are detrimental to themselves and to other people. Don the cloak of integrity and put protective arms around one another.

Become My personal representative acting for Me within the physical world to educate by example and to remove ignorance. My teachings are a windfall of good fortune for those who are eager to learn and then transform themselves. For those who do not care to become involved in their personal enlightenment, I will wait until they finally understand the need to get going with this important obligation that everyone has to themself.

The lack of clearly observing oneself is the main obstacle in interpersonal relationships. In general, people are likely to cringe when forced to recognize a shortcoming of which they are ashamed. People tend to feel reduced in stature when pressed to recognize their personal deficiencies.

It is an uncomfortable feeling to acknowledge one's weaknesses, so the tendency is to turn a blind eye and refuse to admit that they exist. Covering up one's deficiencies is like putting on a blindfold to keep one's self-esteem intact. This common defense is pointless and does nothing to correct character flaws.

I require those who reach for Me to become realistic instead of self-deceptive. It really does not hurt to say to oneself, "That's right. I am not perfect, and I make mistakes. However, I am on my way to improving myself, and I must know what needs to be improved, or I will not reach my destination. I am going to identify my shortcomings and apply myself to overcome them. I will not hide from myself, too weak to own up to my negative behaviors. I hereby empower myself with determination to face myself as I truly am and then transform into a better way to be. I will do this!"

From taking this step and moving forward with constant watchfulness to accomplishing notable progress is only a short distance but one filled with impulses to go back to the old way of doing things. This is when most people fall out of My plan for their education. Determined students who persevere during the beginning stages will find that, after a while, they lose their reluctance to acknowledge their faults.

Then they begin to delight with new discoveries of their shortcomings and relish the challenge of doing away with them. What was once a shameful acceptance of responsibility becomes like a game that is fun to play. This action of admitting shortcomings and correcting them is powerful and psychologically supportive to each individual that takes it.

Once this self-correction process has been in place for a while and progressing well, the next step begins to form. One begins to understand the true impact they have on others. They factor other people's perspectives and requirements in with their own.

The first step automatically leads to the next when a person commits to following My educational plan. The main person that needs to be educated is everyone's own self, personally, privately and honestly. This may take years unless a person firmly focuses on their self-advancement and is determined to succeed in record time. Most people get started and then fall back into their previous comfort zone, which does not encourage comfortable life experiences, since in confrontations with other people, it still always seems to be the other person's fault.

I would like every one of you to be satisfied at the end of your life that you have achieved your ultimate goal of doing the best you can to incorporate My qualities and attributes into your self-expression while you were alive. I explain people's typical behavior with the intent to move you toward this goal. By having what is apparent to Me explained to you, it will move you along more rapidly and ease the discomfort of continuing to unknowingly hang onto undermining attitudes and behaviors. If you follow My guidance, you will be directed to alter your course of instinctive behavior, thereby averting continuous repetition of endless errors.

Since people tend to run and hide from the tough task of knowing themselves with complete honesty, I suggest that everyone run toward their comfortably tucked away faults and misjudgments and reveal them only to themselves.

This is a private exercise. Confessions are not beneficial. Talking about one's faults does not eliminate them. Only personal determination to flush them out by identifying them and then short-circuiting their repetition is going to be effective, and this will undoubtedly take perseverance. The payoffs will take time to develop, but it sure will feel good to be authentic with one's self.

Life is short, as most elderly people will confirm. Putting off the most important task of a lifetime, the reason for being alive on Earth in the first place, is not a wise decision to make. Can you imagine repeatedly incarnating to learn basic lessons that are preventing your evolutionary progress and then repeatedly failing to advance? There is more to experience than repeating the same misguided behaviors that keep one from graduating from the primary school of Earth. Resolving now to live an enlightened life based on My teachings will speed your evolutionary progress and foster My palpable presence within you.

Once you delve into the challenge of becoming self-aware and focus on implementing corrections, the rest comes together over time, and much of it is automatic. It is like growing to adulthood. Get a good start by learning to walk and talk and learning the rules of life. Then as you follow the rules, you develop from stage to stage until you reach adulthood. Get a good start by following My rules, and the rest flows naturally. I want every person on Earth to reap the rewards of inner joy and happiness that come with My expanding presence within you.

I am not a God of retribution and punishment. I am a God of love, patience and compassion. Silently I wait for My children to catch on to My way of being, but this assignment has turned out to be more difficult for them than I would wish. On Earth, learning from one's mistakes is not necessarily the obvious way to proceed. Repeating mistakes is more the custom, although many, many people are dedicated to drawing close to Me. Many want to please Me by worshiping Me, but they are not aware of what is most important to Me.

Loving one another under all circumstances is what is most important to Me. Not bringing harm to any other person is another of My most important requirements. Being patient and respectful is another. I have a long list of preferences for My children's conduct, but none is more important than to love and cherish every other person.

If I can persuade My children to follow My educational plan, each of them will draw closer to Me, even if they are not sure if I really exist. Some think that I cannot be, and this truly does not matter to Me, for I know that somewhere along the way, if they follow My instructions, they will have the proof of My existence that they require. They will detect My presence existing within themselves. They will know that I am inspiring them to take the right actions. It will be instinctive for them to be as I am.

Everyone who takes it upon himself or herself to study the teachings that I am imparting and implement them to the best of their ability will be improving, but there will always be more: more tenderness and compassion to extend, more support to give, and more friendship to share. **I am an extending God. I extend outward, ever increasing My goodwill and support to all My children.** I want all of My children to feel towards each other as I feel towards every one of them, and to put loving arms around each other, as I have placed My loving arms around each of you.

CHAPTER SIX

YOUR INNER DIRECTION FINDER

No one's life is worth wasting. Everyone's life is significant, even when circumstances may be extremely disheartening. Life challenges come in all varieties, causing disruptions that one would prefer to avoid. No one gets away scot-free without their fair share of discomforting life experiences. Some of the greatest heroes are those who stay the steady course and deal with their life challenges one by one as they arise, giving their full effort to doing the best they can to remain positive and keep going. The same circumstances that can cause someone to give up and commit suicide may induce another person to dig a little deeper to get through the challenging time.

I do concede that in certain cases, it may be justifiable to end one's life deliberately. I do not condone extending one's life to be subjected to harrowing suffering from which there is no recourse. In these cases, there is justification in considering alternatives to endless suffering.

People must be honest with themselves if they are thinking about ending their life. They must assess their situation rationally and not be seeking to solve a problem by bailing out when life is trying to teach them a lesson. Many a person who contemplated committing suicide but who had the self-control to push that impulse aside found that their seemingly severe problems dissipated even before their funeral would have taken place.

Acting without carefully analyzing one's situation and the repercussions that will arise because of their actions is common. A quick solution to that, which one wrongly perceived as an insurmountable problem, has taken the life of many a spouse, teenager and others who were destined to enjoy productive and worthwhile lives after their extreme difficulties passed. Would one dismiss their life's value and hurt those who love them the most on a whim? One would think not, but this is exactly what frequently occurs when people commit suicide.

Many decisions that people make during their lifetimes are especially meaningful and require a higher level of knowing beyond what they normally possess. Unapparent to nearly everyone is a God-given benefit that can help people when making important decisions. Within each person resides an inner direction finder to aid him or her when making significant determinations. Some people instinctively access their inner direction finder, but most people only access their mental/ emotional state before making critically important decisions. People who lead very successful lives are more likely to be accessing their inner direction finder, this God-given gift that lies within every person.

Your inner direction finder is within you, and it turns on automatically whenever you need to make an important determination. Know that it is there to give you a push in the right direction. Then do not ignore what your inner direction finder presents. Pay attention to the pull you feel inside to choose a certain course of action, even though it may not be what you initially had in mind.

Great inventors and other creative people tend to access their inner direction finders more effectively than most people do. They are used to allowing their inner creative aspects unobstructed flow into their consciousness. There is a distinct but fine line between one's inner creative aspects and one's inner direction finder, although both exist without restrictions of time or space, and both access a deeper level of inner knowing that does not have to follow the rationality of one's mind.

One's mind makes determinations utilizing one's background, education and experience but weighted to the person's natural decision-making inclination. People generally make determinations that are a mix of enlightened thinking and sheer stupidity with varying degrees of each. When accessing one's inner direction finder, the best answer bypasses the limiting factors of an individual's typical problem-solving capabilities and delivers a pure, best direction for them to follow.

Tap into your inner direction finder by turning off your usual, instinctive decision-making process. Relax your body and disengage your mind. Be open to receiving whatever comes to you without hitting your panic button.

When you tap into your inner direction finder, it may lead you to a course of action that may not be what you would have anticipated. Instead of becoming uncomfortable with the unexpected insight and attempting to override it, look for the reason behind the insight. In an instant, you may have one of those "ah-ha" moments of direct realization that you have hit upon the best solution for your conundrum.

Your inner direction finder has the capability of leading you in the right direction as you lead your life. If you do not know how to proceed when you are at a crossroad in your life, consult your inner direction finder but be sure that you do not interfere with the results it gives you. If you are trying to decide which of two job offers to accept and your inner direction finder indicates one over the other, but that job pays less, it might be tempting to set aside that information. Do so at your own risk, for the inner direction finder has access to information beyond what is available in the here and now. Once you use it successfully a few times and have its results verified, you will proceed with confidence when accessing this mostly unrecognized tool.

Here is an example of the need for using one's inner direction finder to take the higher road in life. In your world today, it is common for those in positions of power over other people to behave brutally in certain instances. Third-world countries in particular, but in other countries as well, there are those who deliberately and cruelly undermine the well-being of certain other people. Those who act against humane standards for all people are especially in need of learning to access their inner direction finder, which would point them away from acts of violence and cruelty.

Internally present within people is the proper impulse to do only good during their lives. This is loaded into every person before being born, but in many cases, it becomes buried under the rush of the senses after birth.

After being born, one's senses turn outward, and the inner knowing of what is important and how to determine the right path to follow may sink down out of consciousness, but even so, it remains within every person. I am encouraging everyone to go deep within himself or herself to touch into the pure essence at the core of his or her being.

Do not let outward appearances or history define who you are to yourself. Become conscious that you are perfect in your natural state, the state in which you existed before you were born on Earth with all the distractions and the extreme focus on everything that is physical. Living on Earth does not reveal who you really are in your natural state. You are going to have to find this yourself by connecting inwardly to the god-like core of your being. Your inner direction finder is your link to the authentic self within, which enables you to bring to your outer world the innate wisdom that resides within every person in his or her pure state.

Do not look to the outer world to give you all of the information that you need. The outer world can lead to mistaken priorities and actions. Rather than basing your behaviors on what you see exhibited in the world around you, seek internally for the pristine intelligence within and let it direct your outward life. Instead of copying what other people are doing that may not be serving the higher purposes intended for people who call Earth home, go straight to your internal direction finder to discern the more worthwhile choice of action. It is greatly beneficial for everyone to access their pure self within and take their cues on what to do from the divine intelligent source that lies within every person.

One's inner direction finder is there to help each person find their way through life by integrating their higher inner intelligence into their life decisions. If everyone consciously accessed this wonderful aid to living, the whole world would change for the better. Utilizing one's direction finder would tend to prevent poor decision-making that leads to harmful actions, which spiral out of control, creating misery and suffering to one's self and often to others as well.

I give My unrestricted support to every person on Earth, which each of you takes advantage of every day. I provide the elements that your bodies require to function, and upon Earth, I provide food sources and life enrichment resources, as well as spectacular landscapes and varieties of plant and animal life. I do not restrict movement from one place to another. Everything on Earth is available to everyone.

Humanity takes My formula for granted without catching on that I want all of you to do the same for each other that I do for all of you. You may think that to live this way is impossible for this reason or that, but truly, it is not. The one and only obstacle to modeling yourselves after how I am and what I do is what you have been seeing around you since you were born, without recollection of what it is like between lives when you are in the higher dimensions. You do not comprehend that all you take for granted is My generosity being made available to all of you to partake of, but also to teach you the right way to be.

If I were like human beings, I would pick apart and judge what other people do, and then I would let that make Me irritated and vengeful. I would put on My happy face when I got what I wanted and sulk when I did not. Everything would be judged, and I would be happy or sad depending on what was going on around Me.

> I am unchanging. I am the way I am all the time. Nothing makes Me turn against one person or another. I see beauty in all people even when they may not follow My standards. I know what lies at the core of every person, which they do not recognize. If people knew that only goodness existed at the most elemental core of every person, their view of themselves would change.

In any endeavor, only if one has the innate capability born into them and has been properly trained can they realistically ascend to the highest levels of achievement. Every person who accesses their inner composition without degrading it by taking their cues from what they see going on in the physical world can become as accomplished as the most outstanding example of humanity. This innate potential lies within everyone, but people do not focus on being as I am enough to dislodge the negative impulses that they have lived with all of their lives. Very few people come close to actualizing their potential to develop themselves as god-like people.

Vigorous dedication to self-education using My principles as the teaching tool is what every person requires. This training begins as one by one My principles are understood and integrated into a person's habitual behavior bringing inner comfort and joy, as well as enlightenment. Whoever achieves this mastery will demonstrate My teachings and serve as a visible role model for the rest of humanity.

I need partners who will join with Me to accomplish the turnaround in perception, which will herald major improvement in attitudes and behaviors. If the frontrunners start now and apply themselves diligently, expansive enlightenment will spread to all corners of the Earth. Practically speaking, nearly all people should find it appealing to join such a movement, which has the capacity to create an uptrend in the quality of relationships throughout the world.

As I explain the precepts that will bring about evolved perception, I am asking those who are availing themselves of this teaching to work with these precepts internally and to invite other people to join in this critically important endeavor. We need to generate an up swell of determination to create a massive pulling together of all humanity to spread enlightened perceptions and ennoble people's interactions with each other. Each person who joins with Me will receive My personal support.

I am proposing a full-out mobilization of everyone who is concerned about the future of humanity and is willing to stand up and do something about it. Nothing less is going to have enough widespread effectiveness in creating a worldwide cleansing of people's negligent attitudes and behaviors. Knowing what to do is the best catalyst when there is a perplexing problem that needs solving. Many people all over the world share deep concerns about the safety of humanity and are willing to pitch in to play a part in creating a worldwide safety net. I will lead, and I expect people who care about the future of life on Earth to follow.

I consider the following to be of major importance for everyone: clean air filling your lungs when you breathe, healthy food and clean water to consume, smiling faces welcoming you and no distress about your safety. In addition, I would add fairness to all people, helping hands outstretched to give aid when needed, protection from abuse and freedom to express your individuality.

In a perfect world, those with plenty would share instead of hoard their excess, every person would be warmly welcomed and cherished even amongst strangers, and everyone would share a unified commitment to support the good of all.

I am saying that all of this is achievable with your combined commitment to make planet Earth a congenial and respectful place to live.

Every person contributes to the world family, even outsiders who feel alienated. Those who feel left out for whatever reason are still important members of My world family. I am in everyone, including those who feel disconnected from the rest and unlovable. No one escapes My loving embrace even though many push Me away and fail to see evidence of My presence around them.

When your eyes are closed, it is hard to see what is right in front of your nose. Now I am going to lead you through an exercise to clear mistaken notions that may be keeping you ignorant of My presence surrounding you. Follow My instructions which will expand your perception.

Begin with thinking about how you got here. The miracle of birth brought you into consciousness. You arrived as a newcomer with intelligence, a mind of your own, and the power to move forward to decipher what this life is about and what you can do that appeals to you. You have free will and ambition and personal power despite circumstances that may have led you to believe that your power was restricted.

Over time, you developed a sense of self despite restrictions put on you. These restrictions interfere with proper thinking and, therefore proper self-evaluation. If left to decide for oneself what one's thoughts and ideas are without outside interference from other people's erroneous misinformation, each person would have a more positive, enlightened view of themselves.

> Erroneous ideas and teachings that come from outside sources send many people adrift upon a dark sea of disturbance. Families, peers and religions are powerful influencers, both positively and negatively.

From an early age, adults teach children what to believe and accept as truth. Much of what they present to children as truth is adulterated prejudice and misinformation. If you took two prejudiced people and washed the prejudice out of them, they would begin to experience each other more benevolently. When prejudices no longer exist, hearts and minds open to other people without restriction.

Prejudices are a heavy load to carry through life, yet they pass from generation to generation as if they were a priceless treasure. Is it not true that nearly all of the religious entanglements throughout the history of the world are due to prejudiced people who feel righteous and superior, acting to eradicate those who chose to recognize My presence differently? There is a presumption of rightness that comes along with prejudice, a self-awarded elevation that has no validity.

Being prejudiced invites living a disquieted life, for one keeps the internal agitation of their prejudice fed with displeasure. Prejudice feeds internal discord and may lead to taking unjust punitive action against one's victims. Look at the history of the world to see endless examples of prejudiced retaliation against innocent people. This is a heritage, which some people still too willingly accept.

Prejudice is not the only roadblock to healthier relationships with all other people. Another destroyer of compatibility is inequality. Many people all over the world are disadvantaged. The ones with the advantages want to hold on to what they have, while disadvantaged people need a helping hand from those who are holding on tightly.

I would like for each of them to change places for one day. The disadvantaged would love to have relief from their constant problems, and the advantaged would learn enough about disadvantaged people's problems in that one day to loosen their purse strings and become more generously supportive to those in need. The best education is to walk in the shoes of another.

In lieu of changing places for a day, I ask all people who are rating themselves as being superior because of the quantity of their assets to truly become superior in My eyes by sharing their excess to create improved circumstances for as many people as they possibly can. If all the wealth in the world was evenly distributed, no child would go to bed hungry, and all impoverished people would feel like they were finally playing on the same team as everyone else. Wealthy people have a great opportunity to embrace putting their money to work where it will provide a much-needed leg up to those who are struggling.

Piles of assets do not build good character within oneself, but using one's assets to promote the well-being of people who have not had many breaks in life most certainly does.

On the scorecard of life, accumulating money is meaningless but what does have significance is what one does to help another in need. I am singling out wealthy people because they have the capacity to perform miracles for multitudes of people. I am also acknowledging that personal acts of kindness and generosity from all people have a markedly beneficial effect as well.

One by one, many more people can receive the assistance they need from friends, relatives, charities or compassionate benefactors who reach out to lighten their load. People, in general, need to become much more willing to come to the aid of other people who have life problems that they cannot solve by themselves. There are people everywhere who can use various types of support, some of which are not financial. The tenderhearted usually are the first to respond to the needs of another person, but it is within everyone to feel compassion and the desire to do whatever one can do to help another.

All people have love and compassion within them, even those who have masked these aspects with their other characteristics. No one is completely good or completely bad: all people have a mix of favorable and unfavorable characteristics within themselves. There are degrees of wholesomeness and degrees of unfitness, and people can choose to emphasize their wholesomeness and diminish their unfitness. A great way to grow in wholesomeness is to act charitably toward people in need, and by all means, do not ever take advantage of someone who is down and out by paying them less than you would another who is in better circumstances. This action is particularly abhorrent to Me.

Always respond toward others as you would prefer if circumstances reversed and you were the one who was in need of assistance. Put yourself in the other person's shoes and feel what they are going through. Do not think that you cannot afford the time or the money to lend a helping hand.

In a reversal of circumstances, a helping hand in a time of need would prop you up and touch your heart deeply. Who would want to pass up the opportunity to give this gift to another person? Life is short, and one of the reasons you are here is to generate as much caring and respect for other people as you can.

Everyone can use a kind ear to listen to their problems or someone to joke with to make light of the demands of life. Laughing is one of the best remedies for the blues and sharing jokes or stories that are humorous brings across-the-board delight. Even something so simple as taking time to connect with another person with humor, finding something to laugh about together, makes their day and yours a little brighter.

This is a wonderful habit to get into. Find more things to laugh about and then share smiles and laughter with those around you, those you know, and those you have not met yet. Open the door to daily delight and make yourself happy to be alive.

I hope you are taking note of what I am telling you because all that I am conveying is important. You may think that you completely understand the points that I am making, but I am looking for confirmation that you truly do understand enough to integrate My lessons into your actions on a daily basis. I am involved with each one of you but especially those who take into their hearts and minds what I am saying. I want action, and I want immediate action. I want to see a vast improvement in all people's behaviors and relationships.

I am eager for the many personal rewards you will receive by being an A+ representative of My presence within you.

The part of Me that is within every person expands as they become more like I am. Eventually, everyone will catch on to this better way to be, but now especially, I need visible representatives who will teach by example. I need to have people in action displaying what My attributes look like and how successfully they work to bring forth the humanity in being human.

Do not think that every single person is not a candidate to represent Me. I do not read resumes or require experience. I require commitment and the effort to follow through with the commitment. This commitment is from you to Me, and the benefits flow to all humanity. Reading My instructions is very easy compared to actually performing an inventory to discern yourself accurately so you can begin to model yourself after Me.

Your commitment sets you on the right path, but making progress on the right path will take careful, honest self-evaluation as you go along day by day with the determination to interrupt those behaviors that undermine your character. Repetition anchors one's behavior and it is a mistake to think that implementing improvements is going to be easy, for when one is not paying attention, the old behaviors automatically take over. This is not a commitment to make if you do not have the determination to endure a long back and forth process. Only those who are strong-willed and eager to be as I am will be successful. Even if someone were not yet to the point of making a full commitment, I would still encourage him or her to go forward, dipping their toes into the water of commitment until they can make the decision to jump in all the way.

> Believe Me when I say that within every single person on Earth are myriads of their particular positive and negative traits and behaviors.

No one is immune from having these within them, and the challenge is being ready to tackle the negative traits and behaviors when they pop up. Do not take excuses from yourself, and do not ignore the traits and behaviors that you take special pleasure in having even though they are not constructive. Clarity and self-discipline are most important for you to employ.

I am making this process sound difficult because it is going to be challenging, and I do not want you to be surprised at how hard it is. It is common to think that one can implement correction immediately. Some things are easier to do than others, and changing one's traditional approach to the way they think and act is like lassoing a runaway impulse.

There is nothing tangible to grab onto to stop it, and one must determine to face down the impulse every time it shows up and overpower it using strong determination. You cannot pop a pill to get you to the finish line of your better way to be. There are no shortcuts, so you will need to utilize utmost control and determination.

Now, something I have not mentioned yet is that the personal rewards are beyond your ability to comprehend without going through the process and experiencing them. The change in one's feelings alone is reason enough to go through this process. As a person implements corrections, elevated feelings start to manifest. They just appear. They are intermittent at first, and then these uplifted feelings remain for longer durations.

A growing sense of well-being stabilizes one's emotions and makes it easier to keep progressing along this path. One feels harmony within their inner world, and they experience serenity, which is especially noticeable when they are alone. Experiencing this deep inner peace is manna to one's soul.

These occurrences are an indication that one has made notable progress and is now reaping personal rewards. Leading a tranquil life becomes especially appealing and is quite a change for many people.

Over time, as more and more people choose to engage in My program for the education of humanity, joy will spread around your world. Everyone on Earth will be relieved over the calmness that is more prevalent. Workplaces will reflect kinder attitudes, and there will be more fairness in compensation.

There are no downsides for any of the Earth's inhabitants. Wealthy people are not destined to become paupers. There will be no hardship involved for those who participate in equalizing opportunity for those who are disadvantaged.

No one needs to pepper their lives with lavish spending on themselves. There is only so much one can provide for themself without going over the line into excessive consumption. With financial excess comes the assumption that one inherently deserves their good fortune, and it does not matter what they do with it. These are not necessarily accurate assumptions.

People make their fortunes in a number of ways, including some that are inherently destructive to other people. Undermining the well-being of others for profit taints the money made. Violation of the public good in order to accumulate wealth puts a stain on the gain.

Many fortunes have been made on the backs of human suffering, which is against all of My laws. I require decency and respect for all people as equals to one another. I do not condone accumulations of lavish excess that pile up without sharing with those who require assistance to move up on the ladder of life. Just because one may have experienced good fortune does not necessarily reflect positively on who they are deep within themselves. The prince and the pauper are both dear to Me, and it is often those who have the least that are most willing to share what they have.

Time slips by unnoticed for most people going about their daily lives. Only when those lives become difficult do people feel the endless drag of the sameness of their desperate situation. Impoverished people who desperately need jobs fall into this category. Can you imagine their despondency when they receive rejection after rejection? Can you imagine the relief they feel when someone puts an arm on their shoulder and says, "I'm going to help you find employment. If you need to become educated to qualify for a job, I will assist you as long as you commit to doing the best you can to learn and become proficient".

All of My children have My fabric within them. I do not discriminate, and I am disheartened when My children treat any of My other children reprehensibly.

> I want everyone on Earth to clearly understand that My presence exists within themselves and also within every other person. Whether one detects My presence or is willing to act like My presence is within them is up to them. So far, very few people have any inkling that this is where I am.

Most people think that I am apart from them because they do not see evidence of My presence. Everywhere one looks, they see evidence that denies My presence, and that is because very few people have My qualities and traits exhibiting within them. I am greater than one can ever imagine, and I do not sit on a throne in the heavens judging you. I am holding each of you close to My heart giving you the opportunity to feel My presence and to know Me personally.

I am the only absolute reality. You will realize this as you advance through to the higher levels of development, which will naturally occur. All the superficiality of your current life will eventually only be a distraction. The more you immerse yourself in My presence, the more real and all-encompassing I will be to you. You will deeply feel your relationship with Me supporting your existence.

Sometimes you will not be sure if your thought or idea came from you or from Me. At times, I will speak through you. You will hear the words coming from your mouth, knowing that they did not originate within your mind and stunning you by the absolute all-knowing intelligence of those words.

There is a world of adventure that awaits everyone who is willing to embrace My teachings with genuine dedication, for in time, I will begin to reveal Myself existing within them.

CHAPTER SEVEN

THOUGHT PROCESSES AND DECISION MAKING

———

Precious children, it is time to comprehend who you really are and embody your god-ness. If each of you were living up to your innate potential, there would be no question about your identities. It would be very clear that each of you carries the spark of divinity within yourself.

This spark of divinity displays itself when people are at their humanitarian best. When they live their lives considering the welfare of others to be as critically important as their own, the spark of My presence is showing. When people are scrupulously honest when they could get away with acts of dishonesty, they have Me in their hearts. When people feel good about themselves, even when they may not measure up to the world's definition of success, and their inner growth and development mean more to them than worldly possessions, they are marching to the beat of My heart.

Consider it natural to become as I am. Instead of standing aside from My presence, step towards me, and I will help you awaken your true identity as a child of Mine. Those of you who are not interested in awakening to your authentic self will continue to experience a void between us, whereas those who are willing to utilize My instructions to bring forth their god-ness within will experience an inner stirring, which confirms My presence resident within them.

Be sure to include the well-being of other people in the plan for your life. Many people are down and out, and whatever luck they may have had seems to have expired. They are no less beloved to Me because of their circumstances, and they should be no less beloved to you either.

I instruct you to reach out to them, as you would want someone to reach out to you if you were in their shoes. Be forgiving of their misfortune and do not hold it against them that they have not been able to pull themselves up on their own. Perhaps they appeared on your radar screen as an opportunity for you to grow in compassion and acceptance.

I would like you to revolutionize your world and turn it into a fair place for all people to reside. I would especially delight in witnessing expanded opportunities for all disadvantaged people.

Those who are not disadvantaged have a great opportunity to uplift and aid other people by flexing their compassionate instincts, thereby growing ever closer to Me. I request that people all over the world unite in their resolve to do whatever they can to create opportunities and better living conditions for underprivileged people, most of whom your world turns a blind eye to aiding. Every one of them is precious to Me.

If you incorporate My code of ethics as the standard for your life, nothing will stand in your way of becoming more tolerant, accepting and beneficial-acting toward every other person. I invite you to take the first step. Leap into forming a closer relationship with Me by taking the direct route, which I am outlining. I am within you, patiently waiting for you to notice My presence.

Most people think that I am far away from them or that I do not exist. Look for Me within yourself when you are feeling optimistic and kind-hearted. Look for Me swelling up inside of you when you take time to pause your busy life to take in the breathless wonders of creation with gratitude in your heart.

The spectacular beauty of Earth is not something that happened accidentally. I designed this planet to offer you the potential to live in paradise. I want the best for My children, but I have certain requirements that need to be explained. As I give you the freedom to design your own lives, I require that you give everyone else the freedom to construct their own lives, as well. I set you down in paradise for you to express yourselves without any limitation except to follow My command to honor and respect all My other children. If you do this, you will notice the beginnings of My presence shining through you.

Discord upon Earth comes in large part from two sources. The first source is from tyrants driven to take charge of people and circumstances to boost their power, wealth and prestige. The second source is from people who disturb the well-being of other people by condemning them for not following the personal beliefs or code of behavior that is the preference of those making the judgments. These judgers of other people's personal preferences anoint themselves as experts and attempt to dictate the rules for other people. People who are vindictive judgers of other people's choices, which they find objectionable, are intolerant and dangerous to society.

My normal is extensive, more extensive than many societies allow. There are always those who are determined to limit what is acceptable and what is not, but have you noticed that what is acceptable to them is always what they believe and prefer? No one stands up and condemns their own behavior patterns and choices, but they will hide some of them to keep them from being exposed. I give My children the freedom to express themselves as they naturally are, for My design is within all of them. My only requirement is to act responsibly and do no harm to other people.

I realize that sometimes it is difficult to discern what constitutes appropriate behavior and what does not.

> Behavior, which undermines the independence and well-being of other people, is clearly inappropriate. Behavior, which is vindictive or dishonest, is also wrong. Everyone must avoid any action that undermines the well-being of another in order to build good character within themself.

One's character defines who a person really is. Someone who appears to be successful but has poor character traits needs to go back to elementary school to learn the basics of being a worthwhile human being. Appearances rarely convey the composition of a person.

Being glamorous and in the spotlight may give someone an attractive slant, whereas another person may appear to be plain and not noteworthy. The image conveyed has little to do with one's inner development until the person becomes so highly evolved that their beautiful qualities shine through, combing My presence joined with their own. Everyone has the capacity to manifest My qualities and characteristics as their own once they develop My attributes within themselves.

Why go through life with a pseudo image of who you really are? All of you are in training to become as I am, even those of you who do not believe in My existence. What you may or may not believe does not influence who you really are. My intentions are to set your focus on the objective of bringing forth your inherent divine qualities, which you are not emphasizing as much as you could be.

I most appreciate people who step aside from the human urge to dominate and control, flexing their ego muscles for personal gratification. Imposing heavy-handed tactics and disregard for the welfare of those who are under one's control deteriorates one's character. No position of authority qualifies a person to short-change another person from being respectfully treated. Looking at people eye to eye, instead of down on any of them, speaks volumes about one's personal code of conduct.

People who are reasonable and considerate of others will gain more cooperation and loyalty from those they associate with and those for which they are responsible. To be solid, build relationships on a firm foundation of respect, fairness and sensitivity to people's feelings and positions, even though doing this may challenge what you consider basic common sense. One gains valuable insight when they question how they would feel if they received the same treatment as they dish out to other people.

No one likes a dictatorial person, especially someone who is being dictatorial to further his or her ego gratification. If a person takes pleasure in dominating others, that person is likely to feel weak and wobbly inside. Dominance can provide a mask to hide feelings of inferiority.

The dominant position should go to those who have proven themselves as outstanding leaders who display impeccable fairness and a high degree of competence. The person in charge ought to have high moral and ethical standards and be without an oversized ego.

Keep in mind that being dominant for ego satisfaction leads to a loss of self-esteem when one no longer holds the powerful position.

Self-images can be accurate or inaccurate and are rarely a concise picture of a person's valuable qualities as a human being. Some people are too hard on themselves and suffer from low self-esteem even when they are beneficial members of the human race. Others may feel that they are innately superior to other people, which displays faulty reasoning.

Being worthwhile is a function of how beneficial one's behavior is to themselves and to other people. That is how I define being worthwhile. Power and position do not impress Me. I see right through a person's maneuvering to puff themselves up to seem glamorous or powerful. I greatly respect those who are humble and have no desire to outshine anyone else.

I would not say to first graders that they did not measure up because they do not have the education that fourth-graders have. We know that those who study hard and devote themselves to gaining the best education possible are the ones who advance themselves. I want every one of you to advance yourself from the current level of development that you have gained in life so far to a more advanced level.

Life is puzzling, perplexing and rarely smooth. Many challenges pop up to throw people off balance and test how well they do under adverse circumstances. Some people manage easier than others do. These people tend to have calm, introspective natures. People whose natures are volatile are more likely to get themselves in some hot water before creating positive resolutions to their conflicts.

The first rule of thumb when attempting to resolve conflicts is to turn your bubbling temper down. Clearly state your position and give your full attention to other points of view. This imperatively important first step opens a pathway to agreeable compromises.

Although it is natural to become involved in conflicts during one's life, it is foolhardy to hold onto the point of contention without putting forth every effort to reach some kind of understanding with the other party involved. For those who do not value resolving conflicts and would prefer to stay engrossed in the other party's perceived wrongdoing, life becomes heavy. Lightness and joy stem from throwing off life's difficulties and basking in the pleasure of the moment. People who remain engrossed in the perceived wrongdoing of another give up their opportunity to create pleasantness in their lives. They draw a curtain of misery around themselves while blaming someone else for their disturbance.

The ability to handle conflicts and disappointments and then to bounce back is of crucial importance. The more resilient and determined people are to get themselves back on the right track after undergoing a down period in their lives, the better able they are to recover their forward momentum. There are ways to turn around even devastating turns of events that might not be obvious at first.

Keep in mind that positive thinking can produce more productive solutions to problems than negative thinking or just feeling sorry for oneself. People who decide not to be done-in by a damaging turn of events are more likely to improve their situation than those who become pessimistic or give up trying. Positive thinking generally creates better solutions than negative thinking.

Do not forget to include Me in your decision-making process. Take the opportunity to talk to Me and tell Me your problem and ask for a solution.

I am not saying that I will solve everyone's problems, but I am willing to intervene in certain developments to perhaps place a thought in your mind that you will think came from you, which turns out to be valuable. I can also send others to you who have solutions to offer that might assist you. I can perform all kinds of services for My children, but I do not want to nullify their responsibility for making sound judgments and good decisions. One of life's goals is to sharpen one's ability to make constructive decisions, well thought out and most likely to produce the desired effect.

Racing through life at a breakneck speed to do everything that one can possibly do is not going to be as satisfying as one might believe it would be. The quiet times provide a respite from the busy world and an opportunity to clear one's mind. The race to accomplish blurs everything that is going on because one's mind is always on to the next event.

To savor life to its fullest, it is necessary to reflect on what is most dear to you as you go along: what you want to remember at the end of your life when you are looking back at what transpired and appreciating it again. Life experiences that include loved ones and especially beloved children as they are growing are among the most gratifying moments in people's lives to take in fully at the time they occur. People's lives move swiftly, and the richness comes from beautiful relationships with family, friends, and other relationships, including one's relationship with their self.

Your self is not a car that you get into to drive here and there. Your self is the essence of your being that transcends your accomplishments and your experiences. Your self is a combination of awareness, intellect and understanding, all of which require peaceful time to integrate and evaluate. How can you know your self if you do not pay attention to the internal changes and the expansions that are taking place?

Racing through life is as if you are trying to stuff too much into a suitcase causing everything inside to wrinkle. I advise those who are living their lives at a breakneck speed to slow down, even to a stop for a while, and spend time thinking about who they are underneath their external appearances and achievements. Sometimes I tap a person on their shoulder and divert their life's course to give them the opportunity to be alone with themselves for a while. Their family members often become concerned when their loved one quits their job for no apparent reason and does not want to do anything other than sit in the sun to think and daydream.

These actions may indicate a fertile time in this person's life as they connect into deeper levels of the essence of their being. They are nurturing themselves from within. After these respites, the person may decide to completely alter their life's direction, or they may go right back to where they were before. In either case, this person delved into a deeper level of experiencing himself or herself separately from the exterior world.

I cannot overemphasize the importance of being alone in nature to leave the world behind for a while. Your world is really an illusion that provides a stage to enact one's personal drama. The stage and all the drama that took place upon it will disappear with one's passing from this learning experience. It is good to step aside from the continuing drama of one's life and exist in the moment surrounded by birds chirping, clouds changing formation, and without any sense of time or need to hurry. I urge you to allow nature to nurture you and keep you more grounded in reality than you think you are when you are leading busy lives.

Regardless of one's position in the world, every person has the potential to be a pillar of moral and ethical goodness. No one is beyond installing the highest standards within themself, even when they have had deficiencies in the past. What pleases Me most is when people who have not had a good record of moral and ethical behavior become determined to change for the better. One's character development is the true measure of a person's success during their lifetime. My goal is for every person to focus on improving his or her personal code of ethics to include what matters most to Me.

My first requirement is for you to develop absolute honesty with yourself. Do not perform a cover-up by hiding from yourself your true intentions, which are really motivating your choice of action. Do not tell yourself that you are acting beneficially when you are not. Truth-telling with yourself is of primary importance and will alleviate causing you trouble when what you would mask as beneficial behavior causes you, or those you hurt, to suffer.

Wrongdoing comes home to roost, so be certain that you have impeccable standards and ethics. My next requirement is for you to think of the other person as if that person were you yourself, and in your interactions with them, treat them only as you would like to be treated. In other words, do not have two sets of standards: one for yourself and one for another person.

Only bring down on someone else that which would be acceptable to you, as well. I target this admonition toward people in any kind of relationship: parental, sibling, marital, employment, governmental and all others. Do not do to others what you would not want them to do to you. Fastidiously following this requirement would prevent most potential conflicts from stewing into a boil.

> My third and most important requirement is to honor and respect all other people, as you would like them to honor and respect you.

If people everywhere disciplined themselves to integrate this requirement into their standard code of conduct, there would be a sigh of relief generating from people everywhere. A world populated with warm-hearted generous-spirited people would not be predisposed to employing intimidation, force and cruelty. Efforts to get along with other people would include inviting them over to talk about and resolve differences in an environment where everyone puts their best foot forward to consider the needs of all.

If people follow these three requirements, the knots that twist relationships would be untied, and the world family would be moving toward universal compatibility. Consider your world. Does it not look like improvements are necessary?

I am giving you the enlightenment that you need to transform the unevolved world in which you live. Flexing muscles and building one's power base does not hold a candle to reinvigorating respectful attitudes and loving concern for all people. Your world needs every one of you to become actively involved as ambassadors of loving concern for people everywhere.

I am certain that all but a small percentage of you are willing to do your best to increase peace and harmony in your interactions with other people. Clearly, some people are not interested, but they are in the minority. Unfortunately, often the minority wields power over the majority when the minority is of evil intent.

People of evil intentions empower themselves and act aggressively to push their self-serving agendas using force, manipulation and deceit. The more empowered they become, the less they consider the consequences to anyone other than themselves. There are numerous examples of great harm imposed upon innocent people by evildoers who act to promote their agendas without concern for those they crush.

I have a proposal for every person who wants to stabilize relationships around the world, making them more beneficial for all people. Nip the bullies in the bud. Do not be persuaded to support anyone that espouses violent attacks against innocents, and do not delay in standing up in opposition to anyone who tries to convince some people to hate or act against the well-being of other people.

Upon Earth, those who have a strong impulse to dominate and control often ruin the lives of some of My children, who are doing their best to survive under oppression ruthlessly brought down upon them. Innocent people who do not include violent acts as part of their nature have little recourse to halt an aggressor's intrusion into their lives. Self-empowered ruthlessness destroys the well-being of both the predator and the victim. Both lose their sense of humanity.

Everyone upon Earth needs to abide by My standards of conduct and preserve the well-being of all people without exception. Those who have tendencies to dominate and control need to rein them in and redirect their attention to gentling themselves. No one has My approval to undermine another person's well-being and especially not in order to satisfy one's craving to exert power over others.

I instruct you to treasure every other person, for each is a part of Myself. Hold yourself as being part of Myself, as well. Behave as I do, with loving compassion and understanding.

Fondness for all of My children fills My heart. I am overjoyed to witness the refinements instilled within people who are dedicated to improving themselves. All people matter to Me, and I abandon no one regardless of their past history. Everyone is capable of rising above his or her level of ethical development achieved so far.

I encourage everyone to use caution when performing his or her personal progress report. I am not happy when people feel like a failure because of something they did in the past. I know how life experiences and the background that one grew up in can turn people in ways that they later regret. I understand the self-loathing in which some people become stuck. I do not want anyone to despise themselves for what happened in their past, but I do want them to strive mightily to overturn their negative impulses.

Putting a halt to habitual behaviors that are detrimental to the development of one's character is the first step, and it is a big one.

Past conditioning leads people to automatically think and then act in certain ways without going through the process of specifically examining the value of what is routing through their minds. I suggest that you take one hour of any day that you choose and pay close attention to all the thoughts that tumble through your mind. If you do this, you might be surprised at the repetitiveness of many of your thoughts that dart in and out of your mind and realize that much of what you think is a repetition of what has echoed through your brain before.

People need to instill a gatekeeper to either allow or block these seemingly automatic thoughts based on their ability to lead you forward in a positive direction.

Do you wear dirty clothes when you want to look your best? Neither should you leave tattered thinking in your mind when you decide to upgrade the quality of your thought processes and decision-making.

Understand that all actions begin within a person's mind, even instinctive actions. Your mind creates a path for you to follow. Deliberately consult your mind before initiating any action and be pure in your intention to create only that which is truly beneficial to oneself and to other people as well.

Do not allow any other objective to interfere with your reasoning process, and that includes propaganda that you may have been exposed to from any source that does not adhere to My standards of conduct.

I want everyone to think independently, to instill only the highest standards of conduct within themselves, and to be immune from persuasions from those who espouse violence, cruelty or dishonest acts of any sort. Be your own gatekeeper. Allow only the most honest, decent, fair and honorable intentions to exist within your mind and use these to direct your course of action. Do not become anyone else's patsy to perform vile acts for any trumped-up reason. Act as I would act. Let this be your standard.

I want every person on Earth to know Me as I truly am instead of relying on contrived definitions of how I am. I am not as many of you believe. I am not a disinterested observer of humanity. I am close to every one of you, cheering you on and supporting your educational plan for yourself.

Each of you made a plan for yourself before you were born, and now you are testing your competence. You may want to ask yourself what grade you would give yourself if you stood aside from your life, viewing it as if it were someone else's. Would you be impressed with the quality of your concern for the well-being of other people and your actions to support their well-being? Even those with whom you are not personally acquainted? People who do not look like you or act like you? How about personal standards of conduct? How pristine are they?

I do not expect people to think alike or act alike. I greatly enjoy variety, and that is why I give people the freedom to be their unique selves. I enjoy seeing how My beloved children elevate their lives by using original ideas and inventions to initiate benefits for all people. I care for all of My children and want all My children to care for each other as well.

Use your imagination and picture a world where everyone has enough to eat, clean water to drink, a job and a safe place to live. People who are inventive and

other-minded can dedicate themselves to achieving this goal for humanity and be part of the movement to act as a support to each other. There are unlimited ways for people to help others. People helping people is My preference over some overly helping themselves to excess while others do not have what they need to thrive.

CHAPTER EIGHT

YOUR EVOLUTIONARY PATH

The core of yourself is not what you access when you overfill your days with hectic activity. When your list of responsibilities is enormous, the tendency is to keep going at a heightened pace to do your best to keep up. The part of yourself that runs around hurry-scurry is like a top that spins and spins until it loses momentum and falls over. Who wants to give up serenity and peace of mind until they spin out of control?

I am offering you this education to enable you to have a clearer picture of how unenlightened people blunder through their lives, inevitably preventing themselves from evolving. My goal is not to criticize humanity but to give every person the opportunity to gain a sense of direction. Most people are in rudderless boats, reacting to where their lives take them instead of deliberately navigating their own boat to peaceful shores of fulfillment. Recognize My instruction as the blessing that it is, and keep allowing Me to instruct you.

There are three parts to yourself. The physical self, which most people think of as their entire self, is the only part that is materially evident. In addition, there are two other aspects, which most people usually do not consider.

Your spirit body houses all of your feeling and thinking aspects and is invisibly contained within your physical body. Your spirit body contains the true essence of yourself. If you were to close your eyes and feel the essence of who you are, you would be sensing your spirit body unless your physical body was squawking at you as it would if you were in pain. When you are in touch with the essence of your self-ness without physical identification, you are feeling your spirit body.

The other part of yourself is the fragment of Myself that resides within every person. In some people, this fragment has become expanded to major proportions whereas, in some others, it may seem that their fragment of Myself is missing, although this is an impossibility. Every person and I are connected, and I am conscious of this connection even though you probably are not aware of it.

I am able to monitor your attitudes and behaviors even though you rarely detect My presence. You cannot hide from Me. At times, you may hide knowledge of your mistaken perceptions from yourself, but you cannot keep Me from knowing you as you are.

I am the observer who is rooting for each of you to reach your optimum level of personal development. If you knew what this would look like and how good it would feel to you, you would set this as your immediate goal.

Hardly anyone actually reaches their optimum level of personal development, and most would be surprised that they might be able to measure up to these standards. Most people take things as they come and do not think about what they could achieve if they put forth a more determined effort.

Take, for example, someone who is going along, taking what life has to offer, and feeling good about how they are doing. They may feel very self-satisfied and on top of the world. What is good enough for that person is not good enough for Me. I want that person to strive every day to rise up to conducting himself or herself as if they are My representative to the rest of the human race.

Do not settle for personal mediocrity when you can blast yourself out of mediocrity and go for personal excellence. This is not a competition of one person's ability to out-achieve the rest as if they were performing in an Olympic event. I want people to out-achieve how they were before when they did not realize that their purpose in this life is to reach the highest degree of evolutionary development that is possible for them to achieve.

Why waste the opportunity that you have to fly high in the establishment of a solid core of My principles? You are here living this lifetime on Earth, and now is the time for you to determine what you are going to show for yourself when this life concludes, and you give yourself your after-life evaluation. I guarantee that you will not be too pleased with yourself if you did not hold yourself to the principles that I am teaching you.

Having this lifetime to advance your agenda of raising your perceptions and behaviors to match Mine is a gift that too many people do not use. Have you ever received a gift that you did not think you would like, so you set it aside and forgot about it? Your lifetime is a gift, even if it does not seem like it is because you have difficult challenges. I urge you not to set this gift aside but to use the gift of your lifetime to overcome the urge to stay rooted in how you have been instead of learning better ways to be from Me.

I am within you, monitoring how you are doing and looking for signs that you are advancing your life's objectives, which you determined before you were born. Most of you have no idea that you made a plan for your life before you were born. Almost everyone has as part of their plan the elimination of certain behavioral aspects that seem to be stuck like glue within them, lifetime after lifetime, and which they would be relieved to remove.

Take, for example, a quick temper. Some people have a temper that shoots straight up into the stratosphere when they get out of kilter. They do not even have time to think about reigning it in. Off it goes doing its damage repeatedly.

If this sounds like you, pay attention to My suggestion. Since I am within you, as you begin to realize that your temper is going to flare, switch the thought in your mind from whatever offended you over to My presence being within you. Even if you are already starting to blow up, grab ahold of yourself and repeat within your mind, "God is with me. God is with me." Even if you do not have a super-hot temper, when yours is heating up use this same approach.

Another good time to key into My presence within you is when something hurtful is about to happen to you or a loved one. Call out to Me with strong emotion as if I were sound asleep and you needed to quickly wake Me up. I respond to commands for assistance, especially when the need at the moment is urgent. It helps to get to know Me personally, so strong connectivity is established between us before you come under pressure that requires assistance. It usually takes practice to instantly connect with Me, so I recommend that we form a close relationship between us without delay.

I am not as far away as people usually envision Me to be. I am a commonly unrecognized part of yourself. I am reachable in times of hardship and in times of sorrow. This is when many people seek Me. When times are difficult, and hearts feel broken is when people are more likely to turn to Me.

When times are not challenging, rarely do people call out to Me. I am not an intermittent God. I am connected with you full time, but most of you do not pay any heed to My presence.

Many of you do hold Me within your hearts, which opens the door for closeness between us. Do not be bashful or think that I would never pay attention to you for this or that reason. I hold every one of you in My always-loving heart, and I want you to expand My presence within you through your own determined efforts.

Turn to Me in times of sorrow, but also turn to Me when your life seems to be going well: you are satisfied and feeling good about yourself. Give Me the call to come closer to you when you are not in a crisis. Some people treat Me as if I were the police department, and I come when there is a calamity. I want you to interact with Me more like the postal delivery person who comes every day.

To most of you, I am an unknown, almost like a fairy tale character in a made-up story. Many of you have a view of Me that is a distortion of how I actually am. I have appeared to be unknowable, unreliable, inconsistent and violent. In times of sorrow when you need Me, I seem to be absent.

You have heard many stories about God's punishments. Many people fear Me because of the made-up stories about hell and damnation. Pseudo-authorities have painted pictures that they conjured up to define what I am like and what I demand. There are too many twisted perceptions about Me, so I do not fault any of you for being suspicious about how I really am.

It is time for all of you to have a clearly defined and accurate description of how I am. I have delayed giving you this information until this particular time in human history when challenging world events seem to be thrusting your planet into unrivaled hurtfulness. Your world is not a sane environment in which to bring forth more children who will have your pile of unresolved problems with which to contend. What makes you think that today's and tomorrow's children will be able to do what you have not been able to do to bring peace and tranquility to your households and your planet?

Human beings have been contentious and irresponsible. They would rather pull apart than forge ahead with practicality and cooperativeness. You tend to be an irrational lot. You do not see what is right in front of your noses, and you have an *It's not my problem* mentality.

I wonder how many of you have thought to yourselves, "Well, I'll be dead by the time planetary disasters strike, so it is not going to be my problem." Do you want your children and future generations to have to solve problems that the earlier generations were too irresponsible to tackle themselves? Are you waiting until the last minute to acknowledge that if your generations had taken better care of your planet and your sisters and brothers upon your planet, your world would not be in the devolving state that it is currently in? You are witnessing the devolution of your planet and of your code of ethics.

Your planet has seen the rise and fall of civilizations but not until now has your planet been in its current dangerous predicament. Not only are there problems in getting along with, respecting and caring for other people, but there is ignorance of the devastation incurred to your planet due to humanity's carelessness. When your planet's putrefied condition will no longer support healthy human life, and then you learn to get along with each other, all will be for naught. An uninhabitable planet does not bode well for the future of humanity.

I deliver My words to you barely in time to avert disastrous, unresolvable consequences to your Earth's environment. Do you have the conviction that after more years have gone by, the Earth will be in a more cleansed condition than it is now? What do you think? If you leave problems unsolved, how could that possibly produce improvement?

There is no unified compulsion from everyone on Earth to demand rational steps to halt the detoxification of your oceans. There has been no unified commitment from your oil industries, your shipping industries and your nuclear power industries to take responsibility to clean up the dirtying of the oceans and environment that they cause. Soon it will be too late, and your populations will be paying a huge price for their complacency.

In general, human beings neglect to appreciate what they have. It is human nature to take a wait-and-see attitude rather than to jump right in to fix a problem that they could let slide. Small problems are far more resolvable than large problems, so why do people allow issues of vast importance such as maintaining a pristine environment on Earth to take backstage to other matters of lesser importance?

People do not pay much attention to matters that they do not see as affecting them directly, and people fail to pull together in a common cause because too many people tend to ride in the boat of pulling against common sense. Many people automatically pull against scientific findings, being hardheaded and blind to what they choose not to see. This passive-aggressive approach to problem solving directly undermines those who are responsibly doing their best to move forward to implement solutions.

I feel sorry for your planet. How would you like to take a bath in dirty water? Her bathwater contains chemical and other residue, oil slicks, garbage and an unhealthy PH balance. Populations have used your oceans as dumping grounds for all kinds of extraneous trash items, which people and businesses refuse to take responsibility for dealing with in a more environmentally friendly manner.

People destroy the gifts that I have given them while being oblivious of the consequences. Many businesses and individuals are shortsighted and irresponsible. If someone gave you something valuable to keep safe and the lives of your descendants and their descendants depended upon this something valuable, you would take this charge seriously. Yet, you leave until tomorrow what is necessary to do today to protect your oceans from becoming toxic and polluted.

You treat your landmasses little better than your oceans. It all comes down to how you feel about supporting and protecting the oceans and the landmasses for future generations. I advise you to keep in mind that you are most likely going to be included in the people of tomorrow who have to put up with the repercussions of the disrespect that you pile upon the Earth now.

The problems that seem okay to leave for future generations are going to boomerang back upon yourselves. You cannot remain confident that in the future, your planet will be sustaining life, as you have known it to be when you are not properly caring for her now. You will return to this planet to continue to work on your evolutionary progress. If you leave behind in your wake disastrous environmental deterioration, you will be reborn to live in the stew that your negligence created.

Earth is at a turning point. If situations do not improve, life on Earth is going to become more challenging. I am supporting you by taking away your uncertainty regarding what constitutes right and appropriate behavior and by removing misconceptions about how I am.

How I am has been misconstrued throughout time, with very few religious representatives professing factual depictions of Me. Some teachings say that I am a punishing god who makes people pay for breaking His rules. Some religious leaders have presented Me as being a god of judgment and damnation, which is contrary to My being. These are some assumptions that people made and then taught to other people, declaring these falsities as a statement of fact.

No one who knows Me would ever say that I am hurtful in any way. No one who knows Me would say that I prefer one person over another. All are My beloveds. Over time, people have attributed to Me human characteristics that are not indicative of how I am.

It is, and it is not, easy to know Me. For most of humanity, up until now, the task has been very difficult because people who taught others how I am rarely had a personal experience of Me. Mainly, their presentations of how I am were based on their suppositions.

People who want to know how I am need to be rational and open-minded. They need to ask themselves if what others have said makes sense. The part about burning in hell to pay for one's sins makes no sense to any rational person. The part about Me favoring certain groups of people over others is another irrational belief fostered by those whose intent is to elevate their theology. I am not saying that there is no place for religion, but there needs to be a cleansing of attitudes and teachings in those religions whose doctrines do not ring true with My direct teachings.

While I am on this subject, I will add that the most direct route to knowing Me as I am, comes from reaching for Me in the stillness of meditation. Mediation is more than sitting still with your eyes closed. During the time when you sit in the stillness, you are opening certain receptors within your brain, which, when opened, will lead you to perceive My energetic presence. You will detect a tingling within your body, and over time, you will reach for Me with certainty that you will tap into our energetic connection. In the stillness is where you will find Me.

Many of you have given up on finding Me through religious practices with an ill-advised doctrine that does not pass the test of rationality. Many people who strictly adhere to their religion do not demand that everything the religion teaches makes sense. They glaze over the parts that they would not be able to swallow if they thought about it, simply because they do not know what else to do.

Either you are *in,* or you are *out.* Moreover, if you want to be *in,* you do not rock the boat by openly questioning the religion's foundational teachings. This is how many religions survive. The faithful ignore offensive or irrational teachings in an effort to prove their worthiness to be close to Me.

I am not anti-religion, but I am against religious teachings that are not pure and valid from every angle. I am instructing all of you to review the dogma of your religion to judge whether your religion is a clean religion. What I mean by "a clean religion" is one which holds true to all of My teachings from every angle and is more invested in teaching the truth of how I am than in perpetuating its own existence.

If you are looking for more fulfillment in your life, I have a suggestion for you. Teach yourself to be as I am. Practice loving every person that you see. Think of them as your sisters and your brothers from the same Father.

This wonderful exercise will expand your consciousness. When you go somewhere, notice the people around you and think to yourself, "These are my sisters and brothers." Then direct warm, loving feelings towards them. Do not particularly search for your lookalikes. I especially recommend that you deliberately send warm, loving feelings to those who appear to be having a hard time in life. Transmitting warm, loving feelings to people overloaded with life's problems helps to uplift them.

You are all sisters and brothers from the same family, the family of humankind. You have recognized yourselves as individuals more than as a family. If all of humanity were to develop warmth and caring for all the other members of your human family, a lot of difficulty on Earth would smooth out. It is the sectioning off groups of people and then judging some as being more valuable than others that sends humanity into a spin.

Everyone deserves respect. It is tough to be minimized and snubbed as being unimportant. It is not easy to hold your head high when others are looking down on you.

I caution all of you to watch your behavior and to monitor what lies within your mind. Catch yourself when you fall into personal behavior that goes against My standards. Going against My standards delays your evolutionary progression and may send it into negative territory for this lifetime.

There are three basic rules for all people who desire to achieve a significant acceleration of their evolutionary progress.

> The first rule is to honor and respect every other person under all circumstances. The second rule is to respect yourself as being equal in importance to all others, neither above the rest nor below. The third rule is to do your best at all times and under all circumstances to demonstrate a high level of commitment to the well-being of everyone on Earth.

There is something that I would like you to ponder – the preciousness of life. Do not think that your life is not worth living unless it is shutting down due to your body's inability to sustain itself. Living with horrific pain or extreme physical degeneration can make life not worth suffering through.

In these cases, you have My permission to release from your body prior to waiting until the very last minute that your body could sustain life. Assisted transfer out of a body that is unsustainable without extreme medical intervention and without any promise of a return to normalcy is preferable to hanging onto the thread of life that remains. It is not against divine law to intervene to end the inhumane extension of a life that has no future prospect of being meaningful.

There are cases of extreme applications of protecting the right to life, such as forcing people to remain alive while experiencing conditions, which make their life not worth living. Setting a person's spirit free to disengage from an intolerable living condition that has no hope of effective resolution is not against divine law. I am compassionate and do not condone extending life under dehumanizing conditions. "Thou shalt not kill" refers to arbitrarily extinguishing a person's life.

Keeping people who cannot actively participate in life bound to their bodies without extending an option to pass on to the next phase of experience is inhumane. Existence does not end. People pass from the physical world to the world of spirit and then back again in never-ending cycles of births, deaths and rebirths until they no longer require Earth experience to teach them right from wrong. Keeping someone captive in a body that is no longer capable of providing the opportunity for expansion of their evolutionary development is against divine will and human compassion.

I am not encouraging people to jump ship when their bodies begin to age. There is a tremendous opportunity to see one's life through a clearer lens with the passing of time. The elder years are ripe with the opportunity to set one's house in order and make amends for past deficiencies. Use the time given to you to your best advantage. Give yourself a leg up on what you have already accomplished by adding to it. As people age, typically, they are more honest with themselves and less protective of their egos. At this point, many people are more capable of taking a frank assessment of their negative aspects, being less likely to gloss over their deficiencies than they would have been in their earlier years.

As people age, they become stronger in some ways. With the lessening of physical acuity often comes pure delight in making fun of themselves and their former egos. Aging strips away a lot of the need for ego embellishment, and people become more true to themselves. Physically aging may not be a picnic, but it provides a rich backdrop for enriched self-understanding, which people usually bypass during earlier stages in their lives.

Every stage of life brings inner growth and expansion of one's self-perceptions. Those who leave their lifetimes early may not have required any more time to complete their agenda. Not everyone comes in with a long list to accomplish. Some cut and run after an abbreviated lifetime, and it is not a tragedy because their short number of years was enough to meet their goals for their lifetime.

Letting go of someone you love can rock you to your core, especially if there was no indication that his or her passing was imminent. People form deep attachments with their loved ones, which makes their loss deeply distressing. I would like to soothe people's feelings regarding the passing of their loved ones. Those who pass from their bodies are still very much alive. They transferred to another plane of existence, where they will most likely enjoy their experiences more than they enjoyed being on Earth.

Without a physical body, they exist in their spirit form, which feels much like a physical body but without the physical body's need for upkeep. Spirit bodies do not get hungry or tired. They do not hurt or age. They remain youthful, vibrant, and very delightful to occupy.

You may pass from your physical body, which suffered from advanced old age or terminal illness, instantly feeling energized and eager to go on. Death is a relief that is to be welcomed when its time has come but not to embrace before you have completed your agenda for this lifetime. Treasure every day of your life, filling it with good deeds, expanded self-awareness and play. It is important to relax, disengage from life's responsibilities and joyfully express yourself. Take time to tap into that child within. Doing this will recharge your batteries and relieve stress. Enjoy life as you go along.

Throughout this discourse, I have been educating you, and sometimes the topics are quite heavy. This is because there is much to convey and a great need to maximize this opportunity to enlighten you. I urge you to incorporate My teachings as a plan for your life. Each of you has the opportunity to advance your evolutionary development now that you are receiving My direct teaching.

I know each of you more accurately than you know yourselves. I love every one of you more than you could ever imagine, and I want to boost your ability to be very pleased with yourself after you pass from your physical body and evaluate how well you performed during this lifetime. I am giving you the opportunity to outshine your previous life performances. Take the ball and run with it. Do your absolute best to rise up to an elevated level of performance throughout the rest of this lifetime.

If you skip out on your obligation to yourself, you will regret it later. There is nothing more disappointing than realizing that you would have done a lot better if you had applied yourself more. I am telling you exactly what you need to know to overcome endless lifetimes spent repeating the same misguided behaviors. It is very difficult for you to perceive the concepts that I am explaining to you by viewing the world around you.

Your world has been teaching you improper conduct, and it is easy to see that life on Earth is not evolving. Respect and caring across the board for every person is only a pipe dream instead of firmly established common behavior. The few who dedicate their lives to uplifting humanity are running into resistance from those who prefer to strut their stuff and push other people around. Egos dominate while common sense is pushed aside.

I am concerned that dueling egos will plow under your civilization. The high and mighty can quickly undo minimal progress obtained slowly over long periods of time. I am explaining elementary concepts that are not commonly apparent to people on Earth. I cannot overemphasize that each person is responsible for evolving his or her own attitudes and behaviors. Your points of view and choices of behavior must evolve to match My own if you are going to uncover the divinity that is inherently within you.

CHAPTER NINE

THE WELL-BEING OF CHILDREN

I hold every person close to Me and love everyone, but I have a special place in My heart for each of the world's children. Oh, how they make My heart sing with joy! Their charming innocence fills Me with delight as I hold all children close in My protective embrace. I would like every child to have parents who are devoted to their well-being and who love their children as I do.

Do not ignore your children. Never ignore your children. Every child is a precious part of Myself that is closer to Me during that stage of their life than they are likely to be later. The spontaneous naturalness within children disappears as they mature. Young children's hearts are wide open to giving and receiving love, and I often express Myself through children. When a child spontaneously hugs you or plants a kiss on your cheek, know that I am expressing Myself through that child.

When people start out in life, the best good fortune they could receive is to be born to parents who adore them and take watchful care of their psychological well-being, as well as their physical well-being. One's body houses that person's psyche, self-concepts and feelings of being worthwhile. Tender, devoted care is necessary for all newborn babies and for all children to experience as they are growing into adulthood. Feeling love instills a sense of security and well-being.

Every newcomer is someone who has most likely been on Earth before and has returned to refine their self and to contribute to the greater good.

Those people who experienced especially positive or especially negative lifetimes during their last incarnation on Earth are most likely to decide to return immediately. Those who had poor characteristics and behaviors during their last lifetime often want to get to work to overcome their past deficits. Those who were good contributors during their last physical life experience are particularly eager to return in order to continue their beneficial contributions. A great number of returnees chose to incarnate primarily to aid the evolutionary progress on Earth.

Every person who is born needs and deserves to be warmly welcomed into your world with endless joy and full, loving acceptance. Each should be securely nestled in the arms of adoring parents and unwaveringly held in high esteem even through troublesome times. Few people can say that they had an exceptionally warm reception from both parents and unlimited support from their extended families when they were young. If they did, they were among the fortunate ones.

> I cannot over-emphasize how important it is to cherish and protect your children. Give them your time, attention and then quick forgiveness when they do not measure up to your expectations. Quiet correction will place them back on the right path. Stern discipline for a minor offense will knock them out of balance and you as well.

Love, cherish and pay attention to your children so when they mature, they will know what loving behavior looks like. A neglected or abused child is not likely to have outstanding self-confidence and sterling character when they grow up. They may be able to work their way out of some of the worst of the detrimental side effects, but their paths will not be as smooth as they would have been had they experienced a lovingly supportive childhood.

Children are a gift to their families, even families overburdened by having another mouth to feed. Each child carries a divine blessing within them, a blessing shared with their families. Every newcomer is someone who has most likely been on Earth before and has returned to refine himself or herself and to contribute to the greater good. A great number of returnees chose to be born again primarily to aid the evolutionary progress on Earth.

Every child holds vast potential to act for the common good as they mature into adulthood, but it will take more than growing up to prepare them to be upstanding citizens of the world. In their early years, a child needs to experience respect under all circumstances. This means they must not be humiliated or excessively disciplined for the mistakes they make. When they are in need of correction, be gentle, rational and sensitive to how they feel. If you yell, scream or use violence, you will cause potentially irreparable harm to their psyche. They must feel safe and loved even when undergoing correction.

It is reprehensible to Me when adults come down hard on children. I do not like it when a powerhouse picks on a target that cannot defend itself. Such behavior can result in a severe loss of self-worth to a defenseless child. If you clearly understood how sensitive and impressionable children are, you would never treat them harshly.

Being a parent requires self-discipline, an ever-loving heart and infinite patience. Every parent needs to place protective arms around their children and be their champion. I suggest that every parent relate to their children as their protector, their cheerleader, and as their port in the storm. Over time, positions change. The child will mature into adulthood while their parents age, to the point of requiring assistance for themselves. Your children are more likely to provide for your well-being when you need assistance if you were there for them, front and center, as they navigated the early years of their life.

Most people find some fault with how their parents treated them when they were children. It is difficult to be a perfect parent, but those that set being a wonderfully supportive parent as their intention are going to come closer to satisfying that goal. Approach parenting as a skill and not an impulsive reaction. Practice remaining calm and supportive even during challenging times.

When children are teenagers, the best thing you can do for them is to build their self-confidence. Notice everything positive that they do and praise them. Stay close to them, and be sure they feel your support as a constant in their life. The teen years are difficult times for many children, and the last thing they need is adults crushing their emerging self-confidence.

Teen years are stop and start years. Teenagers vacillate between grabbing onto life and expanding their horizons to pulling in, becoming quiet and withdrawn. Typically, they bounce back and forth. Teenagers need time to adjust to all their physical and psychological changes that are occurring. It is a time of feeling upended from how they used to be without feeling comfortable and secure with how they are becoming. What they need most during this potentially unsettling time is patience and support from their closest family members.

At this stage in their lives, they sometimes display signs of becoming a responsible adult, and other times, they act like a spoiled child. This is when they need your tolerance and patience the most. Your goal at this challenging time in their lives is to remain positively engaged with your teenager. Always take time for them and stay close. Too many teenagers set off on wayward paths due in part to troublesome ties with their parents.

Parents who discount their children or do not have a kind word to say to them are being cruel. This puts a dagger in the heart of a child. Children who grow up to become troublemakers most likely did not have loving-kindness extended to them by whoever was raising them. Loving-kindness is as important as something to eat. It nourishes the psyche as food nourishes the body.

People abused as children are far more likely to become abusive themselves. You may assume that anyone who suffered from abuse would be determined to create a positive impact going forward in their lives, but this may be hard for them to do. Abuse modifies a person's psyche. Then heaviness, dreariness and low self-concepts often replace what could have been high self-esteem. A person who has experienced mistreatment, especially as a defenseless child, is somewhat like a helium balloon that has developed a leak. It does not fly as high as it would have, had that leak not been there.

I advise parents not to bring children into their lives until the parents-to-be have grown up themselves. It takes a lot of maturity, devotion and patience to raise a child and give them a great start in life. Children are not like dolls that can be set aside for a while. Children require constant loving care, endless patience and devotion to their physical and psychological well-being. It is a full-time job for those who love their children dearly and are willing to do their best for them.

I urge all parents to do everything in their power to give their children a warm, supportive childhood. Nothing is more important than reigning in your temper. Do not allow your emotions to overflow and crush a defenseless child. Wounded children carry the burdens placed upon them for the rest of their lives. Some may learn to cope and go on to lead satisfying lives, but the shadow that should not be there remains a hurdle that shrunk but did not disappear.

If you bring a child into the world, accept responsibility for that child throughout the child's formative years, and then when they are ready, release them to fly in the direction of their choice. Do not hold them back or disparage their choice unless you have valid reasons, such as doing something illegal or something that would hurt themselves or other people. Their sexual preference is exactly that: theirs. Do not interfere or shun them if it turns out to be unorthodox to you. Accept and respect their natural way of being unless it is hurtful to them or to other people.

I am more broadminded than most people on Earth, and I respect unique sexual expressions as being just as valid as those that are more common. People do not choose their sexuality any more than they choose if they are going to be born right-handed or left-handed. I require every person to receive a full education during his or her many excursions to Earth. Most people have been male and female, heterosexual, homosexual and bisexual in previous lives. I intend for each person to receive a full education of what it is like to walk in another person's shoes.

Children, when loved and cared for, receive the best backdrop for their lives. Self-esteem will naturally grow when fear, neglect or family trauma are not present. Sometimes family traumas disrupt childhoods. These range from the death of a critically important family member, separation from one or both parents, abuse by siblings or any of many other causes. Traumatized children are likely to carry their pain into adulthood.

Keep your children safe and protected. You are responsible for their physical, mental and psychological well-being. Do not create unnecessary disruption within your household, and remain aware to detect any ill-treatment that might be going on unobserved. Usually, you can discern whether a child is a victim of abuse by observing their demeanor. Always stay alert to any possibility of abuse. Be sure to take action to protect your child and any other child who may need you to intervene to put a halt to abuse.

Every year of a child's life magnifies in importance. Every year brings exponential physical, mental and emotional maturation over the previous year. Think about it. Children are born unable to take care of themselves in any way. With constant tending, they celebrate their birthdays year after year, stretching their boundaries of what they can do until they grow tall like their fathers and mothers. With proper parenting, children will develop self-esteem and good judgment, enabling them to take good care of themselves and those they become responsible for when they reach adulthood.

If you want to stand up for your children, love them, respect them and educate them. Give them every opportunity to express themselves in their uniqueness. They need your approval of whom they are to create faith in themselves. With self-confidence, they will not be afraid to stand up for themselves and for other people too. It is far better to give your time and attention to developing strong supportive relationships with your children than engaging in any other activity.

Remember how it was for you when you were a child. If you received consistent respect, you were in the minority. The majority of children receive harsh treatment from a friend, sibling, parent, or another adult. Children can be unethical towards each other. In most cases, the troublemaker was a target for ill-treatment and became imprinted with unfair treatment being a way of life. Do not let the cycle of abuse take root within your family. The consequences can be multigenerational and nearly always fuel flames of despair.

When you discipline a child, remember what it was like for you when you were a child. Few children emerged from their childhoods with all of their self-esteem intact. Especially if you do not agree with the treatment you received as a child, make a strong effort to be sure that you do not repeat what you encountered, which made you feel unsupported. Unbelievably, people abused as children carry a greater tendency to become abusers themselves. That is the kind of imprinting that takes place and then continues the cycle of abuse into the next generation.

In the early years of a child's life, children are delicate yet resilient, and during this time, their sense of self as an independent person is forming. Without any setbacks and with the continued loving dedication of both parents, they will gain the best head start in life. They will likely mature into self-confident adults who are unafraid of going forth to create a good future for themselves.

Today's children will become tomorrow's leaders. What better way is there to prepare them for the responsibilities they will shoulder than loving, protecting and respecting them as they mature into adulthood? The generations coming up are going to share responsibility for what happens to humanity in the years ahead and they need to be better prepared than previous generations have been.

The missing ingredient in your world today is genuine respect for all people. Prisons fill with people who experienced mistreatment as children. A severely debilitating childhood is a handicap beyond all others. It is almost impossible for a child who was neglected, abused or chronically oppressed to grow into adulthood being self-confident.

Victimized children receive a kick in the gut that lasts a lifetime. Rarely do they perform up to their full potential. It is far more difficult to rehabilitate a psychologically marred young adult than it may appear. The roots of their disturbance run deep, and a jail cell heaps more of a sense of failure upon them, punishing them more for what other people did to them than what they did to deserve punishment. Many young persons end up in prisons because they had a miserable start in life.

There is no greater threat to the well-being of a young person than to grow up in a household where abuse takes hold as if it were normal behavior.

> If you know of a child who is targeted for abuse, put a stop to it. Do not think that you should not intervene in other people's affairs when the well-being of any person, but especially a child, is at risk.

Watch out for your own safety and let authorities handle the situation. Whatever you do, do not sit on your hands and allow the abuse to continue. Children need champions who will stand up for them. What happens in childhood will affect that person for the rest of their life.

Kindness and respect will always bring a better result than punitive measures in young people whose life circumstances placed too great a burden upon them at a very vulnerable time in their lives. They may have gotten the short end of the straw growing up because of any number of reasons. Instead of treating them as adults who should have known better, I suggest that they be treated with respect and compassion. This is not to overlook their need for discipline and reeducation provided evenhandedly with a lot of positive reinforcement. Compassion and kindness will always accomplish more than punitive measures.

Prisons detain too many people who did not get a fair chance from the beginning. Often minority families live on the fringes of a society, which does not offer them a place to fit in. They may feel disenfranchised and not part of the population that has a desirable future. Whatever the reason, a large number of young adults fall short of what they needed and deserved to have growing up. Putting young people in prisons is devaluing and may ruin their chance to become upstanding citizens.

A significant number of people mistreated as children lack self-esteem. They turn their backs on themselves and do not realize what they can do that is legal, honorable and ethical to help themselves.

The first step is for them to notice everything good that they do and make a list. I advise them to include the little things that one typically might not acknowledge.

The second step is to turn their attention to finding ways to be helpful to others. These do not need to be preplanned. I recommend that people go through life with an eye toward being of service to other people when the opportunity shows itself.

The final step is to enjoy helping other people.

For those who follow My instructions and stay positively focused on how good it feels to do things for others, their self-esteem will grow as naturally as a dandelion in springtime.

If enough people paid attention to what they could do to make the lives of others more bearable, they would be the leaders in changing the fortunes of untold numbers of people. Instead of exclusively focusing on oneself, be alert and aware to notice and then act on opportunities to bring relief to the suffering of other people. Let this be your dedication and one of the important objectives of your life. Make your life count for more than it has so far by extending the hand of friendship and assistance to those whose needs overshadow your own. Do yourself and them a favor by connecting in a way that will bring benefit to you both.

People's success in life depends upon other people, from the family to the workplace, to the support each receives from their friends and neighbors. I would like all of the Earth to be inhabited by caring, sharing people who reach out with warm hearts and loving minds to embrace all other people. I would like for every person on Earth to know that they are important and that all other people are important and worthwhile, as well. Instead of feeling superior or inferior to other people, I want everyone to feel secure being who they are.

Inwardly, everyone shares the goal of becoming a good person. If you conclude that you are a good person, be sure that it is for the right reasons. Test yourself. Good people are fair-minded and eager to help one another. Their goodness shines forth in their demeanor and their behavior. They hold everyone as their equal and do not look down on other people regardless of their situations. If you are one to casually look down on certain other people, you have yet to learn the primary lesson of life. All people are precious and deserve to be treated with respect even when they may have failed the test of conducting themselves in accordance with My characteristics.

Be My representative and be humane in your treatment of all people. Display My qualities, and you will feel good about yourself. My characteristics are inherently within you and can become as natural for you to express as they are for Me. You came from Me, each and every one of you, and you have My goodness and My deep caring seated within you.

You live a physical life filled with distractions and confusion. For Me, everything is clear-cut. I know what is important and what will advance your character development. Striving to get ahead by bullying, forcing, or contriving is a huge waste of time and a waste of an opportunity to refine yourself. Think of yourself as peddling backward on a bicycle when you engage in such behavior. You will never get to any worthwhile place to be by peddling backward.

Full steam ahead, but be sure you go in the best possible direction. There are circular routes. There are sideways and backward routes. There are flimsy routes, and there are golden routes. I urge you to go for the golden payoff that you will receive by taking My instructions to heart and setting out to implement them.

> Sure, it will be tough in the beginning when you find yourself questioning your firmly held suppositions and convictions that do not jive with Mine. You may try to wiggle out of having to give those up. They may support your ego but not your evolutionary development.

In time, it will not be as difficult, so I urge you to stay with your commitment to yourself. If you do, you will become more grounded in My presence which will greatly support your feelings of well-being.

Most of you did not grow up in a world that was uniformly compassionate and upright. Most grew up in a world of selectivity and discrimination. Children reflect what they learned at home. The rest of their perceptions arise from what they see in the world around them and how that world treats them. With this in mind, ask yourself what the chances are for people on Earth to become more civilized during your lifetime if behaviors remain the same as they have been.

The younger generations of today carry the hope for the future, yet it is highly unlikely that they will be able to do any better than the current generations. Common uncivilized and hurtful actions will not change unless the underlying perceptions that support those actions become enlightened. If the younger generations were educated by Me, and only Me, and they did not have your world as it appears today as a guideline, they would have a greater capacity to create an ideal world for all to enjoy.

I have given you a paradise to live in, but for some people in particular, it does not feel like a paradise. Too many people are treading water, barely able to stay alive, and are without the means to pull themselves up. These people have children, and those children experience ongoing hardship.

Keep in mind that these children will be more prone to seeing the world as a treacherous place rather than as a welcoming and supportive place. When people feel cast out by the rest of society, especially when they are young, they are particularly prone to becoming troublemakers, thereby setting themselves up for punishing circumstances. Many people who are undergoing incarceration may have been upstanding citizens who contributed to the well-being of society had they received love, respect and encouragement when they were children.

Do not expect the younger generations to solve the problems left unsolved by the older generations. Get to work right now doing what you should have been doing from the beginning. Look at other people as beloved sisters and brothers and treat them as such. Determine not to allow anyone to go without the required assistance that you have the ability to supply. All it takes is a twist of circumstances to bring anyone to their knees.

In My heart and in My mind, no one is more precious to Me than anyone else. This is hard for you to grasp, I know. Many people harbor a lifelong desire to be elevated in some way.

What matters most in life is not accolades, although a feeling of accomplishment is supportive to one's well-being. After you pass from physicality and evaluate the lifetime you just completed, you will only be satisfied with your performance if you were cognizant and supportive of your family, your friends and nameless others who you extended yourself to assist during your physical incarnation.

I want you to understand that how moral, ethical and gracious you are tells the story of how you are living your life. The best measure of one's personal success is the positive impact they produce for other people. Humanitarianism brings out nobility in people, and your world is desperately in need of compassionate support for others.

I would like for children all over the world to live in a safe, peaceful environment surrounded by people of high integrity who take time to interact supportively with them. I would like all of humanity to respect and safeguard every child and to intervene if a child needs assistance because they are suffering from neglect or abuse. Be certain not to stand aside when a child is in need of support and protection.

Begin by placing protective arms around all children and then expand your loving attention to include every other person. This is the direct path to My heart, which cares deeply for all My precious children, those who have grown to adulthood as well as those who are in their youth.

CHAPTER TEN

RESPECT

—

Human nature has many delightful qualities. The urge to giggle or laugh at something funny and the urge to express joy and happiness are among the most positive. These self-expressions are contagious and create pleasure in life. When you hear someone erupt in a belly laugh, you cannot help but smile. Human nature has many pleasing aspects.

There is another side to human nature as well. Human nature may be puzzling at times, and doing what comes naturally may blunt one's evolutionary progress. Being arrogant is a good example of human nature going in the wrong direction. From My perspective, being arrogant is the same as going to the market and buying oneself a plastic crown to wear on one's head. There is no indication of royalty with a crown made out of superficiality.

People who anoint themselves as being superior to other people put a brake on their evolutionary progress. Initiating and then clinging to perceptions of one's superiority parks people in an ego rut from which it is difficult to extract oneself. If your sense of well-being comes from feeling superior to other people, you actually suffer from inadequate self-esteem. You would probably be surprised if you knew how many people, even those who have great worldly success, suffer from low self-esteem.

You cannot buy self-esteem. True self-esteem exists when one has no need to puff themself up to meet the outer world's definitions of success and are truly satisfied with who they are. They may be poor. They may be wealthy. The thread of commonality is that they are devoid of the tendency to measure their self-worth through artificial means. One may accomplish great feats or earn more money than a city full of people and still feel insecure and exhibit low self-esteem.

Self-acceptance has to exist for self-esteem to flourish. If you look in the mirror and see a glorified reflection looking back at you, you should know better. If you are one who looks in the mirror and does not think your reflection is good enough, you should learn to perceive more accurately. I am waiting for the day when all people truly see themselves as worthwhile equals.

Let Me ask you a question. Do you think that I sit around observing everything that every person does to keep track of who is performing better than the rest? Would you want to do that? You may have a comparing nature, but I do not. My nature is encouraging. I am like a cheerleader who wants every team to win.

I want every person to reach higher and perform better. Everyone is capable of outperforming how he or she has been in the past. To get started, take time each day to support other people in some way or another. I will not give you a crown, but I will give you My gratitude.

Obviously, most people do not value every person as I do. If they did, they would be more uniformly gracious to each other. Generally, people choose who to be cordial toward and who to ignore. For the most part, this is common behavior, which happens frequently, and you have felt how pleasing it is to receive a genuinely warm reception, as well as a perfunctory reception, or none at all.

I am your Creator God, and I have brought forth people of every design, each of whom is unique and dear to My heart. Do not look in the mirror and think that you are either inferior or superior to anyone else. All are My beloveds, and I want every one of you to place loving arms around every other person. Shake off the separators such as skin color, income level, religious perspectives and apparent degree of success in life. Do not place obstacles between yourself and others.

People who receive respect are far more likely to respect other people. Treating criminals as if they were less than human does not encourage their rehabilitation. You cannot treat a person with disrespect if your goal is to teach them to become a model citizen. Think about it. If you had to undergo incarceration in dehumanizing conditions, would it make you loving, kind and considerate?

The goal of penal institutions should be to maintain criminals away from other people while those who did not follow an appropriate code of conduct undergo an educational program. Make the environment restrictive but respectful and humane. Teach by example. Forget the retribution and focus on education and the higher principles that lead to becoming an evolved person. Prisons can become similar to the Reeducation Centers within the heavens. People remain detained until they prove that they can mingle with other people without causing harm to anyone.

Few people are born with evilness inside of them. Most incarcerated people within prisons went off the right track because of parental neglect or inhumane treatment. Others have crafty minds and enjoy outmaneuvering the rules and regulations of society. Selfishness and greed undermine morals and ethics and lead some people straight to the prison's gate.

Anyone who is satisfied making their way through life without taking what is not theirs, does not deliberately undermine another person's well-being, and is determined to respect laws and regulations, is unlikely to end up in prison. People with insufficient morality and a fool hearty attitude are likely candidates for incarceration. Fortunately, even they have the potential to establish exemplary moral standards when respectfully taught what they failed to grasp, which led to their incarceration.

Within the fabric of humanity lies vindictiveness. Being cruel to one another and feeling justified has created horrific circumstances for those targeted. Typically, targeted people are not equipped to defend themselves. Historically, women and children have been easy targets for ruthless people. Minorities are easy prey, and there is a huge history on Earth of callous treatment of minorities. There is no one as dangerous as an empowered evil person who is hell-bent on beating up other people.

> The payoff for casting maliciousness upon another person is the loss of one's humanity. An inner sense of worthlessness sets in as the person becomes dirty to himself or herself.

They often attempt to cover their inner unrest by upping their hurtfulness. With every act of disrespect for the humanity of another person comes karmic indebtedness.

In the case of people who thrive on being inhumane, they will end up being tortured in the afterlife by reliving every cruelty they imposed upon others, personally undergoing the impact of what they dealt out to other people. Only do unto others that which you would have them do unto you. This sums it up. If you want to create good circumstances for yourself going forward, maintain a pristine code of conduct throughout your life.

It is far preferable to act graciously and include all others as your equals, but many people live lifetime after lifetime stumbling when it comes to including all others as their equals. Human nature has competitiveness within it. I gave this to humanity to help you strive to develop yourselves to higher and higher levels of excellence. My intention is for people to compete with themselves to improve. I want you to compete with yourself and score how well you are doing now in comparison to how well you did in the past.

It is up to every person to strive to move up the evolutionary ladder, and that means becoming more *we* oriented instead of *me* oriented. Loving, helping and extending one's self to benefit another pleases Me and gives Me hope that more and more people are catching on to the fact that humanity is inherently divine.

> You will feel the flow of divinity within you when you go out of your way to stand up for someone who is receiving unfair treatment. You will feel the flow of divinity within you when you include all people in your loving embrace.

This does not mean that you need to go around hugging everyone you meet, but it does mean holding your heart open and being willing to be My representative to other people, especially those who have a need you can fill. By extending yourself to others, you raise yourself up to a higher level of self-expression. Your lives are opportunities given to you to stand tall in your support of one another.

I love helping people even when they do not know that I sent the assistance that they received. I am always on the lookout for good fortune that I can deliver to people. Sometimes they have asked for My assistance. Other times I surprise them. Always, I am delighted when people deeply appreciate My gifts.

Many of you have deeply ingrained humanitarian instincts, and you greatly enjoy extending yourselves to help others in need. You act as I do. You are My partners who love unconditionally, as I do.

If all the people in the world who have great financial excess decided to apply their excess to alleviating the suffering of others, your world's poverty would diminish. Stuffed in the pockets of the super-wealthy are vast financial resources, piling up as a tribute to themselves. Impoverished people are often more likely to share what little they have than the super-wealthy who prefer to hang on to what they have as a hollow tribute to themselves.

Real satisfaction in life comes from being a positive force for good in the world. People who stockpile their wealth, instead of using most of it to alleviate the discomfort of impoverished people, are missing a giant opportunity to make an outstanding contribution that would probably be the hallmark of their lives.

My generosity is limitless and readily seen but not often acknowledged. You depend upon My generosity which flows consistently. Do I not provide for all of you in the same manner? You have the sun in the morning and the moon at night. You have fresh air and sunshine and limitless ways to express yourself. Unfortunately, your playing field is not level. Although I give to all, not all receive in equal measure.

Certain areas of your world have more than their fair share of difficulties. There are environmental difficulties, population overgrowth stresses and confounding ignorance about the innate value of every person. There are troublemakers galore. In addition, there are hoarders who get the most for themselves and then sit on the pile of assets they managed to acquire. Mountains of assets do not mean a thing. What does have great meaning is putting those assets to use, making lives better for people who are undergoing severe hardship.

I am in every person. I am experiencing poverty. I am experiencing drought. I am experiencing radicalized people acting abusively, maiming and killing. I am experiencing illness and disease. I am experiencing wickedness in some people and great loving tenderness in others. I am in every one of you. I know your pains, your sorrows and your vast potential to uplift yourselves and keep going even when life circumstances are extraordinarily difficult. I also know how much potential you have to shine brightly with your love and compassion flowing out to others.

If everyone in your world shared his or her excess, poverty would all but disappear. People would be on a more level playing field, and those who were downtrodden would show themselves and the rest of the world that they are as capable as anyone else is. With food in one's belly, decent, safe shelter, and a good education, all people can become equipped to provide for themselves and their families.

> When you provide assistance to others, you are showing Me that you care about Me. When you look into the eyes of a displaced and now homeless person, you are looking into My eyes. When you extend yourself to aid and support disadvantaged people, you are giving Me the greatest pleasure. Knowing that My children love and value one another makes My heart dance with joy.

I am compassionate and generous, loving, kind and resourceful. These are your attributes as well. Do not think that you are any other way at the core of your being. Life's difficulties, including not having been directly taught about My attributes being within you, have kept most of you in a delusional state. You think you are only what you appear to be and that you are limited and not able to do better than you have been doing.

I would like to wipe the slate clean of all past teachings and assumptions. I am hoping that this discourse, which I intend for all people without exception, will enlighten you about who you really are under the current identity that you express.

Realizing the inherent value of every person has the benefit of changing one's direction in life. If the sign says, "Valuable people go here, and those who are not valuable go there," do not think twice. You all belong in the designated area for all the valuable people.

Knowing this is not quite enough to bring out the goodness within yourself. You must also take on the attributes that I am teaching you and use these as the foundation that supports your character. Know yourselves as who you are, each a child of Mine, and express yourselves as I do.

I am a teaching God, and I want all My students to receive an A+ in their life performance. This book that I am presenting is your textbook. Your homework is to apply every principle that I explain to yourself with the intention of straightening out your prior misperceptions, lack of understanding and poor attitudes. There is not one person alive on Earth that fully conducts themself as I do. Without this textbook, you would remain in the dark as you have been, and the evolution of humanity would continue its very slow pace.

Mistaken behavior and attitudes create a complex hodgepodge of hurtfulness in one's wake. The hurtfulness goes unnoticed while the results sting. Other people suffer while the instigator goes their merry way. This is common when people feel justified expressing themselves without paying attention to what they are creating for other people. The self-centered approach to living cuts out one's own culpability in creating distress for others and fosters ingrained hurtfulness within themselves.

The world in which you live is filled with self-deceptive practices and delusions. Many people rate themselves high in their self-evaluation when My evaluation would not concur with theirs. Without developing self-awareness that is accurate and according to My standards, there will not be as much progress being made within each life experience as there could be.

I am not asking you to fix something that is not broken. Everyone needs to initiate a critical self-analysis with the intention of searching for and eliminating his or her faulty beliefs, attitudes and behavior. It is time to stop doing what comes naturally that is not reflective of your divine lineage.

You all have My inherent nature within yourselves waiting to come to the forefront. I am your teacher, and I want you to pass all My tests that come in various forms. There are tests of loyalty, perseverance, fairness, patience and untold others that each of you will eventually score highly on. You must learn the basics of creating non-hurtful, openhearted, supportive interactions with the rest of humanity. I urge you not to delay your move to express yourself as you truly are underneath the disguise of humanness.

Each of you who is willing to pull yourself up to a more enlightened self-expression will become a model for the rest as you act to lessen the turmoil within your world. Your world's discord and the lack of universal respect for all people are fanning the flames of extreme hurtfulness. Obviously, there needs to be a reversal in some people's perceptions of who is worthwhile. To Me, all people are precious even when they do not display exemplary character.

Many teachers will tell you that their students learn best when the lessons are taught with repetition. I am also giving you different angles of perception. Repeatedly, I am presenting My basic teachings to drive home the most important concept regarding the value of every person on Earth.

I show no favoritism. I do not elevate one person over another, and I certainly do not look at worldly success as you do. Piles of money in the bank mean nothing to Me. Hungry people being fed means My children

care about each other, which makes Me pleased. I love to see people respecting and aiding one another with smiles on their faces and open hearts that embrace all other people.

I want everyone to feel good about themselves. The purest way to develop self-esteem is to strive to do your best to be a force for good within your family and the greater family of humanity. This force for good can only appear when people understand what constitutes right behavior and what does not. There are many people who would give themselves high marks as being a force for good when the basis for their estimation does not reflect My standards.

Acting as a force for good begins with purity of intent. If you begin each day confirming to yourself, "Today I will act as a force for good with all the people that I interact with and all the people that I affect in any way," you will be halfway there. Then there is another step in the process. You must be educated in what acting as a force for good really means. Definitions may differ, so I will give you My definition of acting as a force for good.

To Me, acting as a force for good entails having the right perspective from every angle. A true force for good finds ways to step into challenging situations with a determination to resolve problems, conflicts and irritations between people to everyone's satisfaction and without employing favoritism or underhandedness in any way. Reason and respect lead the way to becoming a force for good.

I am an example of being a force for good. I am dedicated to the well-being of every single person. I extend Myself to everyone on Earth without favoritism, judgment or manipulation. If people want to continue to remain in a state of confusion or dissatisfaction, I step aside and allow them to proceed on their misguided paths. I do not force goodness into any person's self-expression. I am the first to respect other people's right to find their own way even when they head in the wrong direction. I do not limit. I support.

I would like all of you to be as I am. Find your own force for good within yourself and let it come forth. Do not try to manipulate another person to do your will. Let them decide how they chose to express themselves. If they create trouble for themselves, be there to pull them up if they desire a helping hand. Otherwise, let them be. Of course, if they pose a danger to themselves or to other people, step in to avoid a calamity.

A force for good recognizes all agendas and sets a course that is moral, compassionate and rational. No caving in to pressure from any source, even one that wields power. Those in positions of leadership will initiate superior decision-making by acting as a force for good, addressing knotty problems and finding solutions without causing damage to any party involved.

By including the gold standard of acting for the good of all in one's reasoning, creative paths to designing plans of action to solve problems may appear when least expected. Too often, people try to solve problems with a restrictive mindset ruling out certain plans of action without going deeper into how modifications may produce a more beneficial effect. When one acts as a force for good, they keep in mind everyone's needs, and they receive flashes of insight about how to proceed to create broad, positive results.

Acting as a force for good opens one's receptivity to flashes of ideas and solutions that never would have come to him or her without their determination to act in support of every person involved. I suggest that you take on the determination to act as a force for good when you begin each day. With this intention, you will set yourself on the path of acting in support of people who may need your help.

Acting as a force for good is the best way to elevate your fair-mindedness, compassion and ethics. What better way is there to raise oneself to a more advanced level of self-expression?

I suggest that you make a list of desirable characteristics that you would like to expand within yourself. Take patience, for example. Nearly everyone would do well to put the virtue of patience on his or her list. Patience is an elusive quality that only slow people seem to have. However, being slow does not equate with patience.

Being patient has two aspects, one external and one internal. The external form has more to do with saving time, such as being impatient for the traffic light to turn green. The red lights always seem to last longer than the green lights, and the green lights are never long enough. This is external impatience, and nearly everyone has a bit of that within him or her. The engines of their bodies want to go faster than the rhythm of their physical existence.

Then there is internal impatience when one wants to do more than they can realistically achieve. Sometimes a child is eager to grow up so they can do more or so their parents will not be calling all the shots. This is more apparent in teenagers who are ready to race into adulthood. Both of these types of impatience are common and understandable.

Then there is another kind of impatience. Self-reflective people tend to become impatient when they find faults in their personal presentation. I am pleased when this kind of impatience brings results such as the determination to improve themselves, but I am aware that some people go too far and berate themselves for their imperfections.

No one on Earth is perfect. All are on a path of cleansing themselves of poor attributes and rising to a more perfected state of being. I do not want anyone to feel that they are less desirable to Me than other people are. Be patient with your shortcomings but do address them with the intention of getting to the point of eliminating them altogether. Be patient, kind and loving to yourself, and know that without a doubt, you will perform up to higher standards of conduct when you set your mind to doing this.

I am concerned about those who do not bother to examine their behavioral traits assuming that they are performing up to an adequate standard. There really is no adequate standard. It is up to everyone to become as evolved as they possibly can become during this lifetime. To do less will bring regret and disappointment within one's self when they look back over their lifetime and realize that they took the lazy way out. To live a lifetime without attempting to improve oneself leads to sizeable remorse when one passes from one's body and realizes how many opportunities to advance their self were wasted.

Patience is a virtue, and I recommend patience when one sets out to reach their highest evolutionary state. No one can ascend to their highest evolutionary levels without equal amounts of patience and determination. Patience and determination together are required to maximize one's evolutionary progress through lifetime after lifetime.

I put you through a very thorough developmental program. There are no shortcuts, however, the rewards are tremendous. Exclusively residing in the highest dimensions of existence without ever having to be subjected to pain, suffering, sorrow or the delusion that some are My beloveds and others are not is the payoff that awaits everyone.

I give life to all, and I sustain life in everyone. There is no extinguishing of My presence within any of My children. I do require all of My children to measure up to My standards and eventually become as I am, which is exactly what is going to occur. Even those who are lazy and do not hold themselves to high behavioral standards will sooner or later desire to elevate themselves to the better way to be. To Me, it really does not matter if you move swiftly to qualify to remain within the higher levels of existence or if you keep rotating back to Earth to face the same challenges over and over again without making exemplary progress.

Your planet is overrun with unevolved people who have no inclination to strive to become better than they were before. Giant steps forward bring the swiftest improvements, but even baby steps will add up over time. If every person made the decision to utilize these teachings to become more as I am, they would turn toward the finish line and be headed in the right direction.

CHAPTER ELEVEN

EARNING STRAIGHT A'S

I am hopeful that the fire to transform yourself into an enlightened being is beginning to flare within you, and you are ready to set your goal on becoming a better person than you have been. You decide. You can take what I am teaching and apply it directly to yourself, or you may remain interested while you are reading but unwilling to go through the effort to transform yourself into a more evolved person. Make a good choice. You are receiving exactly what you require in order to chart a more evolved course for yourself during the rest of your life.

My patience is running out as I evaluate people's conduct. Many of you are letting the lions within you roar instead of gentling them and teaching them good manners. None of you is perfect, and all have a way to go before shining halos begin to appear over your heads. Halos are the result of hard work and determination. They do not arrive gift wrapped and sent to you because of who you are.

The human ego is a wonderful and terrifying instrument. When used to step on other people, one's ego becomes an instrument of destruction. Too many people have an oversized, destructive ego that pounds down upon those they disrespect or those they choose to exploit. Do not dress yourself in an ego garment, for it will not endure. Ego garments rot just like moldy cheese and give off a noxious odor as well.

Dress yourself in a garment of acceptance and respect for all people and disarm any tendency to step onto a ladder of dominance. Suppress any inclination to climb high in order to be the big wig in charge. Too many people stand on a ladder of shaky underpinnings that will not support their egotistical instincts for very long. Power abusers come and go and their moments in the spotlight are not worth the personal decay that arises within their character from how they handled themselves. Blessed are those who serve the well-being of all other people evenhandedly, and as a servant, instead of being a manipulator, primarily focused on personal gain.

If your feelings of self-worth come from how much money, prestige or power you have, you are setting yourself up to experience a hollow, empty feeling when you are no longer a top banana. Consider what lies ahead for those who lose their wealth, power or position when that is how they defined their personal value. If they have not developed self-esteem based upon selfless service to other people, they will feel hollow inside. One can be a millionaire many times over and still feel worthless.

How much more desirable would it be to fill your lifetime with a service mentality? Think about it. When your report card says you have straight A's, will that not be a grand accomplishment?

Here is how you earn straight A's on the report card of your life. You stop making yourself the center of your universe. You include the well-being of others and not only those who are related to you or those who look like and act like you in the construction of your day-to-day life. Think like and act like a benevolent protector of those you interface with or those who come to your attention as needing assistance that you are capable of delivering.

Each of you is a powerhouse of originality and ingenuity. When you put your efforts into solving problems for people in need, the sky is the limit in what you can accomplish. By joining in partnership with other genuinely caring friends, relatives and like-minded people, you can resolve even complex and challenging problems that may initially have seemed to be unsolvable.

Almost everyone has more to give than they are giving to relieve dire circumstances that others are experiencing. Do not use half your ammunition when full power is required. Look around and see what you can do to be a hero to someone else.

Something is very wrong with the world in which you live. Too many people are sitting on mountains of assets clinging to them as a tribute to their worthwhileness. Those excess assets are sitting idle, supporting the ego needs and the excesses of the super-wealthy. Great wealth often, but not always, extinguishes the sharing principle that I implant within every person.

You who live on Earth are sisters and brothers to everyone else. Loving relatives do not sit idly by when other family members need assistance. They jump in to solve problems and offer whatever support they are capable of giving.

If everyone on Earth thought of everyone else as their close relative who they dearly love, sharing would become far more common than it is now, and solving problems for the disadvantaged would expand. Some people work tirelessly to make a significant contribution to the lives of others. Often these people look very ordinary, but to Me, they are the giants among you.

Those in the helping professions such as teachers, therapists, nurses and doctors usually have a heartfelt commitment to serving others. However, they are not the only ones. Engineers, scientists, authors, musicians, students and all other people can have just as much dedication to supporting the well-being of people everywhere, but especially the underprivileged.

> This is what I am after. I want your world of individuals to think of yourselves as members of a very important family. I want everyone to respect and treasure every other person. I want an atmosphere of *"I've got your back"* to emanate from all people towards all other people without reservation.

Living on Earth can be pure hell for some people. Problems abound, and most folks have their share of them. In addition, there are those whose problems are so enormous that nothing of their own doing can alleviate them. This is when I need knights in shining armor to come to their rescue. Every one of you can become such to a person or family in desperate need of support. I welcome your participation as My direct representative to minister to the downtrodden.

"Sign me up." This is what I want to hear from each of you. I want you to go forward to put helpful arms around all those who you can positively affect. Moreover, if you are not positively affecting another person, leave him or her alone. Whatever you do, do not create problems for other people.

What goes around comes around, and you do not want a juggernaut of misfortune developing in your life. There is a boomerang effect when one dishes out evilness to another. It may take a while to manifest, but it will hit hard, and when it comes, you will wonder why this is happening to you.

Be upstanding citizens of the world and do whatever you can to bring about peace, harmony and respect for all persons everywhere. Especially embrace those whose lives have hit a very low point, such as refugees. Do not judge them by the color of their skin or the faith they practice. Look upon all as My beloveds and make them your brothers and sisters. You do not have to be related by birth to belong to the same family.

Another subject I will comment on is the tendency to be too self-absorbed. When people over-focus on themselves and the problems in their life, they make everything harder on themselves. When people over-focus on themselves and how great they think they are, it may take a while, but they will also make things harder on themselves.

Distortions of perceptions waylay common sense and good judgment, keeping people from engaging themselves in a healthy manner. Building a puffed-up ego is blinding. All one can see is bright lights surrounding themself instead of the truer picture of some of the dimness they carry.

Neither think of yourself as being superior nor inferior to any other person, for that is the accurate perception to establish. Do not let your ego overtake common sense. If you need a helping hand from others, feel grateful when you receive it and do not become self-loathing because you could not handle all of your challenges yourself at that point.

People have different rows to hoe. Do not judge yours as an indictment against yourself. Just do your best with your head held high and stay as positive in your thinking as you possibly can. Optimism is always going to produce a better outcome than pessimism, and it is going to keep you more levelheaded so you can identify good options when they come your way.

When people see themselves as being elevated, they tend to put their noses in the air and put their blinders on while celebrating how great they are. There is nothing more potentially dangerous to one's self-assessment than to have worldly success in abundance. People often equate worldly success with superiority. A close look at the lives of those who garner worldly success may show little correlation with superior evolutionary development. However, there are instances where there is a strong correlation, and these are with people who have dedicated their efforts and their fortunes to bringing relief to those who did not get a fair break in life.

I would like everyone across the Earth to join hands together with a commitment to create a better world for everyone, leaving no one out. I would like everyone to develop the instinct to support those who need assistance. This could be something as common as holding a door open for someone who has their hands full or for a mother with small children in tow. Once your gates of perception shine outward to what you can do for another, you will be taking an important step forward in clear thinking and right acting.

I am sad for those who are in the darkness of delusion about their identity and their preciousness to Me. Each one of you is a part of Myself. I know that you do not understand how this could be true. You will know this for yourself when you begin to think as I do.

When you look with approval on those who do not look like you or behave like you, you will be taking the first baby steps. Then when your heart opens wide, holding all people as being precious, as I do, you will begin to feel My tingling presence within your physical body from time to time. You will start to ignore the little things that you may not prefer in other people, and you will become more tolerant and forgiving.

I want each of you to have this experience, which will indicate that you are making wonderful progress along the right path. I have emphasized that I am within you and within all people. I am eager for you to sense this for yourself. I guarantee that you will if you take to heart what I explain to you and advance toward implementing My instructions. Here are some of My instructions.

Be authentically kind and considerate of all people. Feel good about the differences between yourself and other nationalities and races of people. Celebrate the differences and do not use them to drive gulfs of disparity between you. Respect other people's choices and opinions.

Learn from them. Do not automatically think that yours are superior. No one is a king or a queen elevated to a high position over other people in My domain. All are equal in preciousness and importance to Me.

I know of no other way to educate you than directly, as I am doing. My ways have been elusive for most people. Hardly anyone clearly perceives the direct education that you are receiving from Me. There is too great a gulf between My ways and how you commonly behave when you are alive on Earth.

You do not express the high principles of the heavens when you incarnate on Earth. You rely on your instincts and by examining what goes on around you and then mimicking what you observe in other people's behaviors. If you started out in a vacuum, without influence from negative perceptions and actions, all alone with memories of what your existence was like when you were in the heavens before you were born, each of you would shine with pristine goodness. Your big test is whether you can recreate the same goodness, graciousness and compatibility absent those direct memories while you are on Earth.

Each of you tests yourself as you go along, living lifetime after lifetime, with the unexplained objective of bringing out your inherent god-ness within your self-presentation. Dig deep. Pull your inherent godly qualities up to the surface of your being and use these instead of relying on what you commonly see modeled around you. Check your attitudes and actions for behaviors that do not measure up. Then move forward to shine more brightly in the present.

There is more to existence than is apparent while you are living on Earth. One's existence never extinguishes. You may pass from your body expecting the end of consciousness; however, this is impossible. Your consciousness will continue, for I have created you to last forever. You are My beloveds, and I never let go of any of you. You will remain in My heart forever. How could I release any of you from My warm embrace?

You are made in My image, but you are bewildered as to how this could possibly be true. Are you not convinced that you and everyone else are far from being perfect? Rational people who seek to identify their flaws find that there are many. There is little evidence of divine perfection consistently displayed within humanity. In fact, there seems to be an ever-growing overabundance of disregard for the well-being of other people. These are not My ways, so I can understand why people do not notice My presence within every person.

If you only looked at the exterior of an egg, the interior would remain a mystery. Each person is like an egg with a hard shell. Most people look at their hard shell and the hard shells of other people and judge that as their entire makeup. Hurtful behaviors reinforce the hardness of the eggshells and keep the best part of the eggs unrevealed. As people chip away at their hard shells of improper conduct, hurtful behaviors and disregard for other people, the glorious part of the egg begins to appear. Your common goal is to rid yourselves of your shell of ignorance until your true nature stands revealed.

Some of you are making remarkable progress, which I heartily commend. Unfortunately, there is a downturn in evolutionary progress overall. Those, who refuse to chip away at their base behaviors, extend their detrimental impact on whomever they decide to target.

All over the globe, there are larger-than-life examples of outright cruelty and dishonoring of certain other people. In some cases, people who behave in this manner sway others to duplicate their ill behavior. There is an element within humanity that undermines My principles.

Some of you are eagerly advancing your common agenda of evolving yourselves. Others do not pay much attention to the quality of their behavior. Nonetheless, each person is on their own evolutionary path, whether they are proceeding deliberately or haphazardly toward their goal.

Most of humanity has been bringing up the rear. Few are in the lead, and many are meandering somewhere in between. I suggest that you determine, right now, whether to take charge of your own evolutionary development and push it forward or to keep bumping along as you have been.

Your world is not simple to comprehend. I am giving you these lessons because you need them. All of you struggle with moral and ethical concerns, even those who do not specifically think about morals and ethics. Every person has a natural urge to follow some kind of internal standard, even if the standard is of their own making to suit their desires.

I see your confusion and your inability to gravitate to pure definitions of ethical behavior. You allow circumstances to determine your behavior. If you are tempted to take something that does not belong to you, do you not calculate your chance of discovery before you decide what to do? When you are on the borderline of acting without integrity, you had better stop yourself, step back and think twice.

People's desires cloud their perception of right and wrong. You know for yourself how tempted one can become to act a lot, or a bit, unethically in order to obtain the object of their desire. I recommend that you rein in any impulse to cross the line of demarcation between right and wrong.

Circumstances often cloud a person's judgment. Human nature is skilled at manipulating one's reasoning process to justify gaining what a person desires. Human beings are ace manipulators who can solve problems or create them.

When desire runs amok and dictates what happens, people get themselves into trouble. Sure, they may end up with their heart's desire but at a cost to their integrity and their evolutionary advancement. Rarely do people value their integrity as much as the object of their desire in that particular moment.

This is part of the problem. It is more typical to live life moment to moment according to one's desires, rather than deliberately holding oneself to honorable, ethical behavior, which ought to be one's first concern when deliberating a course of action. Be sure that the action under consideration will not cause one to give up high moral ground.

The life you are leading tests your level of evolutionary advancement. Do not give in to your baser instincts. If you do, it will become a habit, and you will undermine your very reason for being alive.

I want each of you to grab on to My teachings and never set them aside. If you want to make this lifetime a rousing success, decide right now to learn from Me. I am doing something I have not done before. I am giving you concise teaching for you to follow, along with explanations and details. I want you to turn your everyday lives into examples of My presence residing within you.

No person is innately more valuable than any other person is. All people are dear to Me. I highly value every person. I will say, however, that those who set high standards for themselves and then strive endlessly to achieve them are an absolute delight to Me.

Unfortunately, there has been confusion over what constitutes highly evolved behavior, with too many people giving themselves high marks that are undeserved. Just because you see no fault in your choice of action or reaction does not indicate that you are being morally and ethically appropriate. Many people make a habit of clinging to this lack of discernment.

The surer you are that your actions are responsible just because they came from you, the more likely you are to be disinterested in knowing the truth. I call this convenient inner blindness. You often see this behavior within people who are in charge of other people.

Just because they have authority, they knight themselves with the right to call the shots as they choose, even when they are obviously exercising poor judgment. You also see these traits displayed in people who act instinctively. Almost everyone has a bit of this detriment within himself or herself, and it is not too soon to get rid of it.

Many instinctive behaviors are common within people everywhere. There is the urge to see oneself as being better than others. This is not an uncommon misperception. The other side of that coin is equally as delusional. Many people feel less important because of many reasons, among them being their lack of razzle-dazzle, which typically comes from having power, position and money.

Ask yourself this question. Do I feel equal in importance to all other people? The right answer is yes, but few people actually evaluate themselves as such. Your world is a delusional place to be, and this is the top delusion that I want to see eradicated.

People who park themselves at the top of the heap and then struggle to remain there are concentrating on the wrong thing.

There is only one top of the heap in My mind, and it belongs to every person on Earth. I hold all of you within My heart. Every person is precious to me, for I see the light of My presence within every person, even those who do not regard being as I am.

Too many people on Earth give up on themselves, but I do not give up on anyone. Do not ever feel less than any other person, nor greater than any other person, even one who has made many errors. Everyone is redeemable no matter how far astray one may have wandered. I want everyone to show compassion and respect for those who have conducted themselves with dishonor. Underneath their exterior presentation is My presence waiting to become expanded within them.

My heart is ever-expanding with love for all of My creation. Be as I am. Give Me the gift of your love flowing outward to all other people. Safeguard one another. Do no harm to anyone. Love and support others, even those who do not agree with your preferences. Do your best not to judge or condemn other people's preferences and choices. You are not them.

Every person is acting from their own perspective based on their particular way of thinking and their life experiences. Some of these perspectives are against reason and common decency. My goal is to educate all of you to embrace and embody My standards of conduct, which will set all people's thinking and acting straight. As this starts to occur, substandard behaviors will diminish, and people will be more inclined to put their arms around each other supportively instead of undermining another person's well-being.

Life is not as clear-cut as it may seem to be to some people, but the rules of life are simple, as far as I am concerned. **Bring harm to no one. Live in peaceful harmony with** all people everywhere. Moreover, always endeavor to continue to refine your perceptions and behaviors to come into line with Mine.

CHAPTER TWELVE

PRESERVING PLANET EARTH

—

When I see people everywhere, I am delighted but also dismayed. There is a lot to celebrate within humanity, but at the same time, also much that is discouraging. I feel like a father who does not recognize some of his children because they are not very much like he is.

As I perceive what happens on Earth, I question whether it is wise for Me to continue to maintain your planet. At this point, I am not certain if I am going to continue allowing your planet to remain home to the human race because of humanity's negligence. Your populations do not sufficiently honor and respect their planet nor their fellow human beings. Wake up and view yourselves as I do. Fledglings. This is what I see; beginners all over the place.

> Your unevolved human race is going in distressing, predictable circles and not grasping what is vitally important for each person to do. Become as I am.

Do you think it is wise to leave humanity on Earth to continue the excruciatingly slow process of developing more exquisite self-expression when multitudes of people suffer daily from difficulties, which could be alleviated by human kindness and caring? I did not create planet Earth to house people who neglect to care for their brothers, sisters and their planetary home. I am not holding all of you accountable, for there are many who dedicate themselves to upholding My standards and practices. There are many who model My behavioral preferences and My attitudes, but this number needs to spread exponentially and swiftly.

Love thy neighbor as thyself. How often do you see this directive practiced? Moreover, with how much consistency? I would like to shine the spotlight on those who are in positions of leadership. They set standards and influence those they steer, for better or for worse. Choosing compassionate and inclusive leadership paves the way for humanitarianism to spread. Choosing leadership that is arrogant and dictatorial rubs off onto those who have tendencies in that direction already.

I am venting My disappointment over the lack of integrity within the human race. There are always brighter stars than others, but My determination is to have mostly brilliant stars lighting your planet, Earth. This is why I am educating you first hand. I want you to know Me as I am, and not in the countless ways that I have been depicted by those who had viewpoints but who did not know Me personally.

I am always loving and accepting as well as endlessly forgiving. There is no thing you do that will ever cause Me to desert you. However, having said this, I am determined to raise your level of performance before it is too late to undo the cumulative harm that poor character and poor behavioral expression have produced.

I implore you to keep your mind from primarily focusing on the misdeeds of other people. This is a strong human tendency, which provides nothing constructive to your own self-improvement. I want you to turn your gaze inward and evaluate yourselves, searching for the most obvious troublesome areas for you to address in order to refine your concepts and behaviors. Wrap your minds around the fact that you are in great need of evolving your individual self and then get busy satisfying this objective.

Imagine what could be accomplished if all people improve their concepts and behaviors, even a small amount. I really prefer that you shoot for the moon and strive to bring about a complete transformation of all your unethical attitudes and behaviors. Relieve yourself of indecent motivations. Do not be conniving and manipulative. I urge you to drop the habit of justifying wrong thinking and wrong acting. Let these be some of your initial goals.

Catch yourself when you start along the well-worn path of twisting and turning your morals and ethics to suit yourself. You can always drum up a justification to do what you want to do that is unethical or damaging to other people. Human beings are great connivers. They can twist the truth and disguise their intentions in many ways that suit their presumed best interests. Good character is lacking within a person who hoodwinks others through manipulation and distortion. Notice how many people there are whose main concern is to manipulate to get what they want.

People use various means to seek approval for themselves, including a tendency to glamorize oneself or one's accomplishments in order to have something to show for themself. When people receive their accolades from the exterior world, they are on shaky footing. Tides turn, and people who ran towards you at one point may lose interest.

Do not ever think that worldly accolades will cut it when you complete your life and evaluate how you performed. At that point, you will be evaluating your behavior, your impact on other people, and what you have remaining to accomplish in order to build a strong moral and ethical base within yourself. If you set only one goal for yourself during this lifetime, decide to build good character. Greatly expand your moral and ethical base, and you will have lived a most successful lifetime.

Nearly everyone yearns to feel good about them self but doing so requires wholesome self-esteem, which does not come easily. Most people struggle with feelings of low self-esteem, which they do their best to cover up. Braggadocio is not an indicator of self-esteem. True self-esteem has the potential to develop only when a person has total acceptance of who they are, despite still needing to overcome their weaknesses. They do not let their weaknesses define them.

Acknowledging one's imperfections without allowing them to define who you are can create a joyful state of self-acceptance that is enormously satisfying. One does not have to be perfect to have true self-esteem. A child who is learning to walk has true self-esteem despite falling down now and then. That child knows he or she is making progress and doing better than before.

This is what I want all of you to grasp. The point of being alive on Earth is to progress from an infantile state of being self-absorbed in one's needs of the moment to progressing through the other stages of development that follow until one reaches the pinnacle of human development. I want each of you to realize what is and what is not important. Power, money, fancy cars, oodles of possessions, the flash and dash of life may be pleasurable in the moment, but these can act as distractions, which sideline you from achieving more worthy objectives.

Be careful not to ignore what you came to accomplish. One's possessions often act as diversions that do not pay good dividends. Be sure to avoid the mindset that your possessions form your status report for this lifetime. One can be on their deathbed, adding up what they accumulated or failed to accumulate during their lifetime without knowing that it really did not matter.

It is not too late to adjust your priorities. Turn your focus from being self-centered to being other-centered as you go along leading your life. Halt any extreme focus on material possessions and go after the important issues such as how to extend yourself to people who have a need you can fill.

Create wonderful deathbed satisfaction within yourself now by taking My advice to heart. No matter how old you are or how many decades you may have left to live, generate acts of compassion and kindness that will give you tremendous pleasure to recount as you prepare to pass from this life.

The pinnacle of human development takes place when one's focus turns to genuinely respecting all other people, acting morally and ethically, and holding this as one's basic code of conduct. I also include contributing to the good of all. When people are not on a clear-cut course of striving to reach the pinnacle of success, as a human being, they bob around going up and down. They exhibit a mixture of positive and negative actions and reactions, which they randomly access. They apply to the current situation whatever suits them at the time.

That is why the human race is not evolving at an adequate pace. How many people do you know who adhere to the same code of ethics and behaviors that are similar to those I espouse? Imagine how much smoother, more enjoyable and safer interpersonal relationships would be if everyone did.

I understand how difficult it is for you to retrain yourself after having the experience of living without instructions such as these. I am endeavoring to catch you up to where you need to be in order to make the most of your life experience. Get to work. Refine your perceptions, attitudes and behaviors. Raise yourself up to a higher level of personal accountability.

I am going to make a decision very soon about whether to close My Earth experiment and remove the inhabitants to schoolhouses that are not on Earth. My patience is running out because I am disappointed in humanity's inhumane treatment of each other. I advise those of you who are ready to discount what I am saying to slow down and take heed.

You may be looking for a way out of having to change your patterns of behavior. When you are on Earth, you think that what you see is all there is. Your perceptions are extremely limited.

I want each of you to know that there is far more to your evolutionary adventure than what you typically focus on while you are alive on Earth. While on Earth, your goal is to build a platform of good behavior and excellent characteristics. You need this platform to support your expansion into other areas of creation that are going to be available to you once you become qualified.

I will not give you more information about what becomes accessible to you after you graduate from the preparatory school of Earth. I want you to keep your focus on coming to terms with your deficiencies and striving to eliminate them from your modus operandi. Serve yourself by cleansing your attributes and perceptions, which run counter to what I am teaching you.

Do not relax and tell yourself that what you are reading is a bunch of baloney. Instead, think about Olympic athletes who train rigorously to reach their peak performance levels. They are strict with their training, and they remain focused on the results they are determined to achieve. Then when it comes time to compete, they perform at outstanding levels that astonish even themselves at times.

I want all of you to put yourself in training to prove that you can be as I am. I would enjoy nothing more than to witness a massive implementation of high principles and behaviors among all people on Earth, but especially among those in leadership positions. Those who make decisions and set policies that intrude on the well-being of some of their constituents are under My directive to treat all people with fairness and compassion and not to subject particular groups to harassment or unfair treatment of any kind.

I recommend respectful, compassionate behavior under all circumstances. People in leadership positions are not the only ones who need to work on their rough spots and edges that interfere with their evolutionary progress. People everywhere of all ages and backgrounds have a lot to address in order to bring themselves more into alignment with My attributes.

Treasure My children's diversity and ingenuity. I want the love, respect and caring that I give to all My children to flow forward. Give to others what I so lovingly give to you.

I will never desert you. You may feel cut off from Me at times but, I assure you that I will still be there within you, even when times are especially difficult and trying, and you do not know what to do next. I request that you remember how you felt when you were going through especially challenging circumstances and now make a promise to Me. Be attuned to what other people may be going through when they are experiencing severe difficulty and then act as My surrogate.

Step into their presence with determination to do whatever you are capable of doing to aid them. Powerfully or lightly. In a troubling kind of situation, even having someone to sit and listen to one's sadness or desperation can bring some relief.

When one is in a desperate state, the presence of someone who cares is a blessing beyond what may be apparent. Helping another to shoulder their onerous load is inordinately uplifting to both the downtrodden person and the concerned other who is willing to assist. If you begin to feel down about yourself, the best thing you can do is provide needed assistance to another person without desiring anything in return.

Selfless service to a person in need is the most personally rewarding activity for you to undertake. Keep this in mind. Have your eyes open for when you can step in to support another person to alleviate their distress.

Share your humanity with others in loving, caring ways. Little things count and uplift all involved. Become someone who is always on the lookout for opportunities to serve the legitimate needs of those who are having difficulties.

I invite all of you to become My personal representatives. Study what I am teaching you. Embrace My ways and show Me that you are making a determined effort to integrate the way that I am into your self-expression. Cleanse yourself of all that is not worthy to remain within your being. This includes your prior self-expression, which requires adjustment in order to become pristine and indicative of your status as My son or daughter. Every one of you is capable of making this transition into a more evolved self-expression. People everywhere must express themselves as they each are, My sons and daughters, and stop behaving as if they have no connection to Me.

If I seem impatient, it is because I am disappointed in humanity's lack of progress. Eons of time have gone by, and what has developed? Superior weapons and more selfishness, greed, arrogance and hand wringing over the state of the world you live in today.

No one seems to know how to solve the problems that become more unsolvable as more and more people lash out at innocent others. Then more people display the same or even more savage behavior. Your world is in great need of refinement instead of copycat dysfunction.

Do not follow the lead of any person who deliberately causes distress to others through an act of disrespect. People who look for ways to press hardship upon others are falling far behind in their evolutionary development. These people will experience deep regret when they have to face their personal deficiencies, taking full responsibility for what they brought about, which damaged another person.

Your world is ripe with people who delight in acting abusively toward others. They do so to entertain themselves and give themselves a heady feeling of how strong they are. These are the weakest among the weak.

Those who push around other people and delight in the damage they inflict are going to have the same thing happen to themselves down the road. I have found that the most effective way to educate slow learners is to let them feel, in like kind, the harm they did to other people. The troublemakers will have to go down the same road and experience the same low circumstances that they brought upon other people, causing them avoidable pain and suffering.

You might be surprised at how many people do not catch on to the necessity of being upstanding in their treatment of other people. Not enough people deliberately carry this intention within them. That which one does to others will come home to roost and influence their own circumstances going forward. Those who treat all others with kindness and consideration feel good inside and quicken their evolutionary progress.

On the other hand, those who deliberately look down upon and cause problems for other people are going to feel wormy inside. Instead of enhancing their feelings of self-worth, they will develop self-loathing, which they will do their best to hide. One cannot hide from inner decay. They will lose their sure-footedness as they provoke disdain among more and more people who eventually will push back, demanding a cessation to ill-treatment. People who cause problems for others may rise high initially, but eventually, they will sink low. Eventually, they will feel hollow inside as they continue to do their best to keep themselves ignorant of their offensiveness.

No doubt many of you can find examples of this offensiveness in your experiences. It is a fact that being in a position of power over other people often brings with it an abuse of power. Power abusers leave accountability behind and often go forth, cutting a wide swath of abuse in their wake. Those affected typically are in lesser positions and fear making objections that might tempt the one with the power to cut them even lower. Pouncing upon people who appear to be weaker will destroy any integrity a person has been able to amass in their previous lifetimes, and sets the stage for their downfall.

Mainly, people are unaware of their own troublesome behaviors. Most people have a big blind spot in their view of themselves. They can pinpoint other people's weaknesses but are blind to their own. This delays their evolutionary progress and keeps them returning to live lifetime after lifetime, riding on the roller coaster of life.

The roller coaster of life does not get a person anywhere. It just goes up and down, thrilling, frightening and repeating. I prefer that one forgo the roller coaster ride and instead takes the preferred way through their life. Go forth with your eyes open to your negative traits working diligently to supplant them with superior traits and qualities.

I created you in My image, every one of you, with no exception. However, you have pulled delusion and separateness down around you, and you are unaware of your heritage. So toss out your clinging to the notion that you are separate from Me. If each of you were convinced that you definitely are a part of Myself, you would more willingly take on My characteristics.

I am dissatisfied with the slow pace of evolutionary progress on Earth. I am greatly dissatisfied with man's inhumanity to their fellow human beings. Devolution of life on Earth will occur unless you implement radical improvements.

You have three big areas to address. The first is the ill-treatment of other people. The holding down of certain classes or groups of people is unjust and places a demoralizing burden upon their shoulders.

The second issue to come to terms with is the arbitrary elevation of certain people over others, which is against My principles. I did not create inequality among humanity.

The third area to address is the future of your planet. You are assuming that your planet will continue to support your populations even though you disregard the importance of preserving her well-being. How polluted do your oceans have to become before you realize that their pristine nature is unrecoverable?

How do you plan to feed your booming populations with enough food for everyone? Who is going to choose who receives nourishment and whose hunger becomes unbearable? These are all questions that you need to come to terms with.

Every person needs to wake up to the reality that you cannot go on living as you have been living and doing as you have been doing. Living as you have been is not going to cut it anymore. Everyone must open his or her eyes to the obvious and acknowledge the disastrous state that your planet is in right now.

You know how uncomfortable it is to ride in an elevator jam-packed with people. Already certain countries have populations that are far in excess of being at a comfortable level for which to provide. Without the basics of unpolluted air to breathe and pure water to drink, living on Earth becomes treacherous.

You think of yourselves as being civilized, but I think of you as head-in-the-sand beings. Instead of planning, many of you live day to day and place your decision-making in the hands of religious authorities who tell you not to limit the number of children you bring into the world. Many of you do not make rational reproductive decisions. You are the ones that then become responsible for the problems and issues created by exponential population growth.

Why would you think you are pleasing Me by bringing more children into the world than your planet can accommodate? You follow church directives from centuries ago when under population was a problem. You surrender your decision-making to ghosts of the past.

Without a doubt, it is more convenient to put off solving today's problems, especially when you do not personally feel the direct impact. A common thought in a person's mind when they hear about environmental concerns is that they are powerless to bring about significant changes and, in addition, those problems are not likely to affect them during their lifetime. People pass off simmering environmental issues as if they were a hot potato that no one wants to hold in their hands.

There are people who cradle planet Earth in their hearts and work to address environmental concerns. They delight in giving hands-on assistance, but there are not nearly enough of them, and usually, they can only affect small improvements. Those improvements, however, can be monumental to the people who receive them. Purified drinking water is a major improvement that many people in undeveloped countries still lack.

The oceans cradled life in its earliest forms. Without viable oceans, your planet will not be a safe place to live. Upsetting the ecological systems on Earth will cause contamination of food sources, water sources and the air that you breathe. You are living in a precarious situation.

Stay as you have been, and you and the rest of humanity are doomed. You will occupy a putrefied planet. You will inhale putrefied air. You will drink putrefied water. In addition, you will not have enough food to feed the masses of people who are too many in number to count. I urge you to consider the consequences of waiting too long to put your priority on cleaning up and preserving your planetary residence, treating her respectfully and not milking her for all she is worth during your lifetimes, thereby leaving her too depleted to continue supporting future generations.

None of you has the full picture of the state of your planet. Many of you recognize no problems at all and think that concerns about the viability of your planet are overblown. If your backyard looks okay, you think that everyone else's backyard is also okay. Even if your backyard is okay now, you have little reason to expect it to be alright in the future. I urge you to stop burying your heads in the sand. Shake loose of the deceptions you have been feeding yourselves regarding the urgency to clean up your planet.

You may ignore what is happening, but the clock is running down on how much time you have to work with before time runs out. You know how you feel when disaster strikes and then you look back and realize that you should have seen it coming.

There is a disaster in the making for your planetary home, and there is not much to prevent this unless all residents pull together in a cooperative effort. The naysayers will have to stop pulling against efforts to target the problems and address them immediately. Be prepared for people to say, "There is not enough money to do all that." It is just a matter of setting priorities.

Every person on Earth needs to do some serious soul searching. What do you want to leave to future generations? You can let today's problems go for future generations to wrestle with, but if you do, the problems will be even more severe and far more costly to remedy.

What are your priorities? Live for today and let tomorrow take care of itself is the irresponsible option you have been living with. There may not be a tomorrow if humanity fails to become responsible citizens of planet Earth.

CHAPTER THIRTEEN
BUILDING DIVINE TRAITS

My dear beloved children, use My critiques to ignite your flame of awareness so you can improve your self-expression and bring to the forefront a strong determination to evolve your individual self. Rise up to your true potential as My offspring to exhibit My qualities within your physical being. I am awakening you from your self-centeredness and teaching you that which is very difficult for you to discern without My assistance.

Most of you are living in paradise, going sideways in your evolutionary progress. Yours is an imperfect world inhabited by people who do not understand the basics of honorable behavior. I acknowledge that there are multitudes who do hold themselves to pristine standards of conduct. These people press forward, always striving to do the right thing and holding to this determination as the guiding precept of their life. They maintain a constant focus on sustaining pristine moral and ethical standards and do not let themselves off the hook of accountability when they disappoint themselves.

However, I am dissatisfied with your overall progress as a species. On some fronts, such as being more open-minded about racial inclusion, there has been an inkling of progress, although not enough to begin to satisfy Me. The distribution of wealth is nearly at a standstill. Most inhabitants of Earth are treading water, staying afloat, but without adequately refining themselves. I planned for the populations on Earth to be more highly advanced by now.

The state of your civilization is disappointing. Humanity has within it the zest to become high and mighty. This urge shows up on playgrounds and in boardrooms. Only a certain percentage of people have this trait, but it is enough to disturb large numbers of people when applied in certain ways.

Consider the ways in which arguments and disagreements expand into exaggerated entanglements. The ultimate expansion is when wars break out over the high and mighty flexing their inappropriate muscles. Look at the history of your world. Much of it reads like a horror story of the suppression of weaker populations.

I am not interested in more of the same. I did not create your planet Earth to become a conflict-ridden world of backward thinking and behaving. I intended for humanity to evolve themselves as they went along. I expected it to be a very slow evolutionary process characterized by forward progress, followed by some backsliding. Right now, I am dismayed because there has not been significant overall progress, but there is a tremendous amount of evolutionary backsliding.

It takes an evolved person to leave their ego out of a conflict and offer solutions that are fair and equitable to all those concerned. Such people are in short supply. Typically, the hotheads prevail, and then conflicts become exaggerated. The main guiding principle of the hotheads is self-interest. All over planet Earth, I witness tugs of war between hotheads who do not want to give an inch of ground to their opponent, even when it would be in the best interest of both parties to compromise.

As I have already stated, I am weighing the pros and cons of continuing to support human life on your planet. I am vacillating at this point because Earth shows some signs of progress but not enough to balance the weight of current unevolved attitudes and behaviors. I intend to wait a few more years before making My final decision. I am giving humanity a chance to measure up to My standards and expectations that have not been clearly explained until now. My goal is to give you the education that each of you needs in order to bring your world into alignment with My principles.

The next step is up to each of you. These are your choices: undertake the task of reforming yourselves, becoming single-mindedly focused on upgrading your attitudes and behaviors to come into line with Mine, or think about it but do nothing. This is your choice to make, and I hope that enough of you take what I am saying seriously.

You do not have much time to dally. In less time than you might imagine, I will make a decision whether to allow Earth to remain as a viable residential option for human beings or to transfer humanity to other areas within creation. Earth is not the only potential home for humanity, but she has been, at least until now, among the most forgiving.

What would you do if you were especially nice to someone and then that person repeatedly acted viciously toward you, disregarding common decency and respect while undermining your well-being? How long would you tolerate the insults? Would you meekly stand by and do nothing, or would you strike back?

No one among you has been as patient, kind and forgiving as your planetary home while you have ignored her well-being and treated her as an unfeeling object. I have news for you. Your planet has no obligation to continue to serve humanity. She has no mandate to sacrifice her well-being for the sake of humanity.

Life on Earth began as an experiment. I wanted to observe humanity's evolution. My children on Earth have all been precious to Me from the beginning when humanity started out. Each of you is My offspring, and I delight in your growth in intelligence and your ability to evolve as you live lifetime after lifetime, learning as you go.

Very few of you are newcomers to planet Earth. Most of you have been here repeatedly. I am gradually refining you into identical versions of Myself. This is My goal for you to accomplish as you live, die and then come back to live again.

Nearly every time you return to live again, you encounter different circumstances but many of the same challenges. Your old bugaboos stay with you until you refine them out of your character. Some people move quickly, reaching advanced states of self-expression before most of the others. Then they do not return, except to aid those who are still struggling to evolve their attitudes and behaviors.

This is why there is so much conflict and lack of respect for other people on your planet. The most evolved people do not commonly return, so the people remaining on Earth are mainly those who have yet to reach an advanced evolutionary state of being. This has become a worse problem than it was before. Those who act out their mean streaks and ruin the opportunity for other people to live and evolve peacefully scald people's lives.

There is a mean streak within humanity. Inflamed egos derive satisfaction from causing harm to others. Some people strive to create an empowered feeling within themselves through the act of hurting other people. In the past, people have had more of a tendency to fight against impulses such as these, and fortunately, many still do. However, more and more apparent are those who act on their hurtful impulses, and in so doing, they ruin the lives of not only the people that they target but the lives of those people's families. Such behavior brings decay into the human race.

I have grown impatient with the lack of civility upon your planet. Although many improvements are being made in some areas, the area that continues to be the most important to Me, humanity's treatment of one another, still lags behind. I want to emphasize that I am not holding all of humanity accountable for the lack of honoring and respecting all other people.

I hold the malicious ones accountable. They are troublemakers who empower themselves by spreading the venom of hate and disregard for the preciousness of all people. I am concerned about the psychological damage these troublemakers induce for My beloved children, those who were directly injured, and those whose hearts ache for those who received the brunt of brutality.

My plan for humanity has been for the evolutionary process to accelerate, but at this particular part of the evolutionary cycle, the opposite is happening. I cannot allow this to occur. I will not allow this to occur. I will not allow humanity to devolve because of an evil strain of humanity that has lagged in its responsibility to honor the rest of humanity.

It is not only those who commit outright acts of inhumanity toward other people who have disappointed Me. All those of backward thinking that stomp down on certain segments of populations, judging them to be inferior, are a grave disappointment to Me. These backward-thinking people put the brakes on their own evolutionary development.

What would you do if you were Me? Would you tolerate malicious treatment of certain segments of populations by ruthless people? Would your answer differ depending upon whether you were the one dishing out the injustice or the one on the receiving end? All too often, people who are in a position to affect the well-being of others have little respect or empathy for them.

I rarely intervene within your world, preferring to remain an observer. I am like a proud parent who delights in his children's progress. Many of you are making Me very happy with your humanitarian instincts. Countless numbers of you are dedicated to uplifting the downtrodden and those victimized by others who disregard the preciousness of every person.

Unfortunately, not enough people devote themselves to assisting those who have a tough road in life. All it would take to participate in making someone's burdens lighter is greater awareness of what other people need and then contributing whatever assistance you are capable of giving. You can also act as a go-between by connecting people in need with other means of support. I delight when people step up to help each other, and I invite all of you to give yourself the pleasure that comes from lovingly extending yourselves through acts of kindness and sharing.

You can see the position I am in. The majority of people go their own ways, not particularly noticing what other people are going through. They have enough on their minds with their own difficulties and focus mainly on them. No one's life is free from having problems. However, if everyone waited to assist others until their life was running completely smoothly, rarely would one get around to turning their attention on how they can elevate the well-being of other people.

I urge you to include the downtrodden, the needy and those whose lives are tragically disturbed by hardship as part of the plan for your life. Become a do-gooder. Always keep an eye out for ways to eliminate hardship from another person. If you have nothing other than respect and a kind word to give, do not hold back. Sometimes it is a simple act of caring that can pick someone up when they are down.

If those people, who are mainly good people but simply not very attentive to looking for ways of helping other people, got revved up with the inspiration to turn their focus to acting as a force for good in other people's lives, your world would brighten appreciably.

Your world is dark with worry, dishonesty, selfishness and neglect. You cannot carry another person's burdens for him or her; however, you may be just the person who can lighten another's load in some way or another when you step forward to see what you can do to assist. If everyone established the goal of becoming aware of how they can contribute to the well-being of other people and then set out to lend their support, your world would sparkle with spontaneous acts of kindness and compassion.

Why live in a world where people, for the most part, think only of themselves and neglect to spread joy and happiness wherever they can? Let spreading joy and happiness be your life's goal and then set out to fulfill it. Extend love, joy and caring as a natural course of your day with a smile and warm feelings for all those with whom you interact. Do you think you can do this? I know that you can if you make this your intention at the start of every day.

Living on Earth is a collaborative effort. No one goes it alone. Every person is interrelating with others. There is dependence upon those who provide necessities of life, such as nourishment for your bodies, health care, clothing, transportation and endless other services and requirements. Each provides for others in some way or another. For the collaborations to work, people need to pull together and perform well for the rest.

If people on Earth had a team mentality, where each performs cooperatively and for the good of all, nagging problems would be solved in genuinely caring ways. As it is now, in many instances, nagging problems expand, while a tug of war goes on between people who see things differently and are not interested in solving problems, as much as in dictating their will and controlling the outcome so they can flourish. Too much *me* and not enough *we*. Junkyard dogs are more agreeable than power mongers who manipulate to control outcomes to boost their authority and fill their pocketbooks.

I have already stated that no one is dearer to Me than any other person. I love all the same, but I must admit I am more pleased with people who see themselves as being equal in importance but not elevated in importance over other people. I do not enjoy people puffing themselves up with hot air to put on a premise of superiority.

I like people to have self-esteem for genuine reasons such as contributing to the well-being of other people and acting with wholesomeness, not elevating themselves to feed their egos. Egotistical people spend their lifetimes climbing a non-existent ladder of superiority. They deceive themselves as they look down on other people who quite often are more evolved than they are.

Your world is full of people who look down on others for reasons that they contrive. I do not look down on anyone. I feel sorry for those who feel less worthwhile than others because there is no "less than" within My heart. I treasure every one of My children, even those who are making grave errors in judgment. Some of My children take longer to catch on to the preciousness of every human being, and yet a blessed few easily recognize this inherent knowing from deep within them. I have been patiently waiting for all of My children to feel towards each other the love I feel for each of them.

Patiently waiting for humanity to take on My traits has paid few dividends. Your negative traits, ingrained within the human psyche, are fortified by common acceptance. Most people have the mental acuity to tell right from wrong, although they hesitate to challenge the inferior moral and ethical codes of their peers.

Be forewarned. If one's peers are bigoted and exclusionary, this behavior has a tendency to rub off on others. People duplicate what other people do. Monkey see. Monkey do. I call this the head in the sand approach to living life.

Most of your world's populations put their heads in the sand by dutifully adhering to age-old policies. Historical precedents should carry no weight when determining right and acceptable behavior from hurtful, wrong or abusive behavior. In your world, accepted beliefs and practices often tend to reflect centuries-old precedents that were not particularly advantageous to the general population. Typically, these precedents originated from those in positions of power who were intent on regulating the masses in a way that was advantageous to themselves.

> Clinging to precedents from centuries ago, which stand against common decency and My command to love and respect all other people, constitutes backward thinking. Keep the precedents that reflect My teachings and reject the precedents that tie populations to hurtful patterns of behavior from the past.

If you are looking for examples of the point that I am making, I have two in particular to mention. The male sex has overwhelmingly dominated the female sex and given little thought to what it would be like for them if they were discounted as being inferior. There has been a propensity within humanity to draw the rules to favor the males.

Look at your world and acknowledge the finagling to keep women in restricted positions where they lack the power and position that males have. Your workplaces and your religions offer an undeniable glimpse of suppressing certain segments of your populations, and often with the expectation that the degraded and suppressed segment serve those who put them in that position. Those who make the rules have a strong propensity to slant the rules for their own benefit.

When religions sprang up, there was an opportunity to hold power. Those that stepped in to organize the followers of the originator of the religion reflected the male dominance that was rampant. Women had menial roles to play. Historically the power grab by male religious authorities demeaned women and held them as second-class citizens. This is still somewhat apparent today.

That which you commonly do to women, you do to minorities as well. In your world, the tendency is to award the dominant ones power, position and the freedom to cause unjustified hardship on those scorned as being of lesser value. This is the inherent weakness within the human race: most people do not highly value all other people.

Nearly everyone, to some extent or another, differentiates between people they consider worthwhile and those they think are not worthwhile, or are not as worthwhile. Then they adjust their attitudes towards other people according to their own invalid perceptions. This is the main detriment to building lasting peace on Earth.

How would you feel if I said to you, "I like those people over there more than I like you? They are precious to Me, but you are not." This does not make you feel very good, does it? Now, can you empathize as some segments of societies discount the preciousness of untold numbers of people and snub them or deliberately bring harm upon them? This should be easy for you to envision as you look at your world today, as well as your history of violence, wars and general disregard for the preciousness of every person.

Your world has always been a competitive place. Competition has positive aspects and negative aspects. When people compete with themselves to rise to a more advanced level of achievement, this is usually a good thing. However, competition for a leadership position, where exercising power over others brings with it the ability to support or crush the well-being of other people, is a tricky business. Most people who crave power are naturally unfit to wield power and authority because they are not other-oriented in a compassionate and fair-minded way.

I want everyone who craves power and position to understand that advancing themselves to the number one slot is not what life is about. Your lives have the potential to build your character when you set aside the urge to compete and replace it with the goal to serve. Utilizing your talents and abilities is your ticket to life satisfaction, but unless you also support the well-being of other people, you will eventually be disappointed in yourself.

Give yourself the shining light of top-notch intentions and actions to build wholesome self-esteem, which is the best internal support you can generate for yourself.

> Each of you is greater than you may appear to be. You each have the potential to expand your humanitarian instincts and to reign in your lack of self-discipline. Forget about how you used to be and become the epitome of what I want you to be. I want all of you to put on your best behavior, even if it does not seem comfortable to you right now. In time, My teachings will anchor within you and feel right and natural.

I understand that My teachings are a big turnaround from standard practices that seem to be embedded within humanity. Do not let this turn you away from taking the higher road in life. If everyone embraced My standards and practices, you would all enjoy more satisfying lives.

There is nothing more gratifying than becoming as I am. At first, you may feel phony as you mimic My traits without having My knowing of rightness naturally within you. Then you will relax, and heightened feelings of well-being will appear with more regularity as you remain committed to being as I am. Without noticing, you will be turned in the direction of taking on My traits gradually and comfortably.

If making this transition to becoming as I am frightens you, ask yourself what you are frightened of losing. Is it anything worth keeping, or is it something you should have done away with a long time ago? What does your self-esteem stand on? Is it shaky and supported by grandiosity or one-upmanship? Do you crave attention and power to throw your weight around and be a big shot? No matter what methods you employ, there is no better way to build self–satisfaction than to become as I am.

Your potential to unveil yourself as Myself in human form is something to take seriously. I am leading you to the highest path you can take during your lifetime. If you choose to cling to a substandard level of self-expression, you will continue to delay your evolutionary progress.

The whole point of living your life is to evolve yourself to become as I am. I encourage you to take what I am saying very seriously. Ultimately, you will be the one to judge your performance for this lifetime, and you will design your next lifetime to teach yourself the lessons you could be learning right now during this current lifetime.

My beloveds, value yourself and every other person as well. This is My core directive to you. Be as I am and never think that you or anyone else is beyond redemption from past misjudgments and hurtful behaviors. In addition, do not take the lazy way through life. Use this lifetime as an opportunity to advance your personal evolutionary achievement.

Set your goal to become the best person that you can possibly be. Use My standards and perceptions as your guide and receive inner support from Me. I do not leave you to do all the work yourself. I stand ready to collaborate with each of you, but you need to show up with strong determination to advance your evolutionary progression.

I am committed to supporting your personal spiritual development. You may wonder how your attitudes and behaviors relate to your spiritual development. To Me, they are inseparable. A person whose life reflects their reverence for humanity is a clear demonstration of being very spiritual.

Each of you is a spiritual being occupying a human body for a while. You are each a part of Me who has no direct physical evidence of our connectedness. You know yourselves separately from each other and from Me, although we are all interconnected.

My spirit fills all of creation. Whatever exists within creation is a particle of Myself. I am clearly visible, but you do not realize what you are seeing. You have been looking for Me apart from yourself.

I am committed to giving My support to each and every one of My children. Since I am in every person, I understand the misperceptions that send people into confused, regrettable behaviors that most do not detect as being unwholesome. It is far easier to keep on doing what you have been doing all along than to stop and reconsider your perceptions and behaviors to determine if they are of high quality or if they need to be brought up to My standards. If it were possible to give you classes and lectures that you could attend, I would automatically enroll every one of you. My words that are being gathered into book form will give you the same opportunity to know My mind.

CHAPTER FOURTEEN

BELIEFS AND ATTITUDES

—

Now I am going to get more to the point. I told you how dear you are to Me. I gave you multiple examples of deficits within human behavior, and I have not demeaned you for having them. I have given you plenty of time and opportunity to wash yourselves clean of your instinctive disagreeable behaviors, and I am growing weary of watching in dismay as cycles of hurtfulness continue unabated.

I did not design human beings to oppose or undermine the well-being of one another. I did not design humanity to pull against or neglect each other. I want your world to be universally supportive to all people.

I expect all of you to do better than you have been doing. In fact, I am going to make it imperatively necessary for humanity to set a better course for yourselves by taking away the safety net that you have come to rely on. I have forestalled dangerous happenings upon your planet that would have occurred had it not been for My intervention, even as I have observed in horror as people annihilate other people with complete disregard for the other person's humanity. I do not want to witness a continuation of evil actions brought to bear upon too many men, women and children, each of whom is dear to Me.

I know what each of you has in your mind and in your heart. Your intentions are clear to Me even when you disguise them in an effort to salvage your honor. Instead of taking the blame for shameless behavior, you excuse yourselves by turning off awareness of the harm you dish out.

You bow down to the god of vengefulness, which provides an excuse for acting on your unevolved primitive instincts. Why else would some people detonate explosives intended to kill groups of people at random? Why do people follow leadership of any sort that espouses harming other people? It does not take many people to disrupt the lives of great numbers of people and turn villages, cities and countries into chaos.

Destroyers of other people's well-being are never going to become heroes. No matter how convinced they are about the rightness of their destructive acts, no one who deliberately injures another person will gain anything but sorrow. Each act of deliberate hurtfulness delivered to any person under any guise, with the exception of self-defense, will have to be atoned.

The worst karmic condition a person could create for himself or herself is to deliberately harm another person or, worse yet, a great many people. What you do unto others will be experienced by you as well. Just because you may not face the snapback immediately does not mean that it will not occur.

> My rule is to do unto others that which you would have them do unto you and be willing to experience the consequences of what you dish out to other people.

People who harm others are very shortsighted. They do not grasp that they have been working lifetime after lifetime to instill good character traits within themselves. The record of all the progress that each of you made because of your good choices and good actions over your many, many lifetimes does not become revealed while you are still alive.

If you received a report of the number of lifetimes that you have lived in order to advance yourself as far as you have, you would not want to squander any of the progress you have accumulated. If each of you had a clear view of how many more lifetimes you would have to live to evolve yourself to the point of freeing yourself from endless repetitions of the Earth experience, you would carefully safeguard all of the progress you have already made. You would hold back from causing a detrimental effect upon any other person and build yourself a pristine record of attitudes and behaviors that mimic My own.

Other options will become available to you once you measure up and no longer have to return to Earth to refine yourselves. Other worlds exist for you to explore, and you will have the opportunity to visit many of them. Your Earth experience is very restricted because I will not accept you flying off to another area of My creation without proper credentials. You have little idea of how evolved you will eventually become based on how you are now. You have a tremendous incentive to refine your attitudes and behaviors, but the incentive has not been apparent, so people tend to meander their way through life instead of making a plan to evolve and then sticking with it.

If you knew what the other worlds are like, you would have a very difficult time being satisfied remaining where you are now. If you saw a movie of what some of the other residential options are within the greater expanse of the limitless heavens, you would dedicate this lifetime to passing every test in order to become qualified to choose a more expansive residential option for yourself next time. It is a big disadvantage to believe that you only have one life to live. It is a big disadvantage to think that Earth is the only residence for people.

I caution you to be careful of what you believe based upon what some religions have handed down. Some organized religions are filled with teachings that run counter to My nature, which is all-inclusive and non-judgmental. People who are attracted to belonging to a religion usually want the answers handed to them instead of trying to discern the answers for themselves. They prefer following a religious structure that may, or may not, bring them closer to Me. Sometimes following this path provides enough satisfaction, and sometimes, it does not provide nearly enough.

> I recommend that you learn to go within to glean the answers to life's mysteries yourself. Those who go within to find My presence will be rewarded. There is nothing that pleases Me more than people who seek Me through meditation. These people are creating a direct line of connectivity with Me, and sooner or later, they will feel My tingling presence vibrating within their physical body.

> My existence is provable, and My closeness to you is palpable. It will take time and effort to reach this advanced stage of development, but every minute of your dedicated effort will pay off as you personally experience My presence being within you.

I look at religions as a double-edged sword. One side is positive, and one side is negative. On the negative side, many people were led astray by following their religious authority's urging to discriminate against those who, in the authority's minds, did not qualify to be valued.

At certain times, some religious authorities have taken it upon themselves to discriminate against, judge and harshly punish certain people that they arbitrarily determined to be unholy. Taking it upon oneself to be judge and jury to those who displease you does not reflect My nature or My standards. Nor does the arrogance that comes with religious righteousness.

There is another problem as well. Religions tend to reflect the customs and judgments of the times in which they were founded. My truths are universal, and they do not change with the times.

I am timeless, and so are My teachings. Man-created teachings are subject to alteration to reflect current attitudes and perceptions. Astute common sense must be diligently applied to all religious teachings to determine if those teachings truly reflect My values and standards.

I am unchanging, and My universal code of conduct for humanity is always the same. Love thy brother as thyself. Bring harm to no one. Extend yourself graciously to all other people. If you adopt this code of conduct, you will be pleasing to Me, and you will be pleasing to yourself and to others as well.

Your world truly does not need the complexity of religions. No one group or another is innately superior to any other.

> I want you to realize that throughout history, religions have been created to preserve the teachings of one of My highly evolved representatives. These representatives are volunteers from the highest parts of the heavens who came to teach in ways that the people of those times could understand. People such as Jesus, Muhammed and Krishna gathered loyal followers about them. From the spiritual teachings that these followers received and passed on to others, three of the world's greatest religions formed.

Along with My direct representatives, there have been others who have set the course for the continuance of these religions and others. Some have represented the initial teachings better than others, and some have completely ignored what is most important to Me and led their followers in the wrong direction. This is why I decided to communicate directly with humanity.

Most religions are based on ritual and historical precedents, which were tweaked along the way. Original teachings, when reliably recorded, were simple and not complex. Those who took it upon themselves to keep the initial teachings intact were few. Other people came along and had their own slants and interpretations.

Scholars created their extrapolations, which they considered the correct interpretation. Conflict arose over what to believe as religions did their best to attract and increase their followings. From My perspective, a great many people walk around with their noses in the air completely convinced that the religion that they follow makes them better than other people.

I will tell you again. Follow My behavioral code of conduct, and you will make Me very, very happy. Love and respect one another. Do whatever you can to aid someone who needs assistance. Know that you are precious to Me and that everyone else is just as precious to Me as you are. Teach yourself to be humble and throw away your arrogance. You will never need it again. If you heed My directive to you, you will be delighting Me.

I am not against religions, but I want people to know that they have to be very careful to hold themselves to all of My standards and not abandon rationality, common sense and seeing My presence in all people. Religions that do not comply with My instructions can go back to the drawing board and institute corrections in order to come into compliance.

It is up to each of you to let go of self-centered religious teachings that puff up their religion as the one and only true religion. No one has the right to award this designation to any of your world's religions. There are many paths for people to follow when they desire to establish closeness with Me, and I will say that being part of a group of like-minded spiritual people who embrace My teachings is very fulfilling. Being in such a group may help to elevate one's closeness to Me.

I suggest that each of you dig deep to get to know yourself better. Much of what people believe they really have not analyzed in depth. Religious beliefs are a good example. I suggest that you ask yourself how well you investigated other options than the religious belief that you learned from your family and may still follow. Did you choose it from several others because you deeply resonated with that religion's teachings and viewpoints? Did you make a deliberate, well-thought-out choice, or did you continue the family tradition because it was what you knew?

If you are living in the Middle East, you are likely to be Muslim. If you are living in India, there is a strong likelihood that you may be Hindu. If you are living in the Western world, there is a strong likelihood that you may follow a Christian religion. How many of you actually investigated other religions before choosing your own?

Do you see what this can create? Generally, people hold those who are like themselves in high esteem. Problems may arise in any area of the world when a majority clings to their belief system and makes life tough for those who chose to follow another faith. It is very easy to distrust that of which you do not have clear knowledge. It is easy to accept that which is familiar and the choice of your neighbors and family members.

If from young adulthood, people studied various religious options and were encouraged to align with the one that they felt most drawn to, people around the world would be more open-minded regarding the religious choices of other people. Then your world would lose a source of conflict. Presumption of the superiority of oneself and one's choices along with the presumption of the inferiority of other people and their choices, is one of the deterrents to global compatibility.

Consider how many conflicts arose because of religious righteousness. This is what the Crusades were about, and those that planned them were ignorant that their own civilization was not nearly as advanced as the one they attacked. How can everyone get along on Earth when people do not honor other people's choices and differences? It is all too easy to award oneself, and those who mirror oneself, an elevated position in one's mind. Doing this displays a lack of respect and personal insecurity.

I would like to take all the people in the world on an adventure trip. I would take them to meet other people who were very different from themselves. I would give each of them three days together without any other people, just the one other person with whom they spent their time. The two of them could discuss anything they wanted to discuss, but I would give them an assignment.

Their assignment would be to get to know the other person and to find things in common with them or things that were admirable about the other person. Then after the three days had gone by, I would ask each of them if they would like to see the other again. In all but a small percentage of instances, asking this question would make each of them smile with delight.

I would also like to match people with others who practice a different religion than they do. I would like to put together a Christian and a Hindu person, a Muslim and a Jewish person, and representatives from all of the world's other religions with someone who adheres to a different religion. I would give them time to get to know each other and have some meaningful conversations. Then I would give them a form to fill out afterward for them to report what they thought about the other person.

Those who paid attention to what the other person was saying and asked questions about the other person's religion would find this exercise to be perception expanding. Those who choose to look down on the other person and do not pay thoughtful attention to what that person said, would complete this exercise with all of their rigidity intact. One has to have an open mind and a willingness to respect other people's choices in order to get along with each other. Religious differences put unnecessary wedges between people when there could be an expansion of perceptions.

People identify others by the color of their skin and their religious practices, among other characteristics. I identify all as My children, and I give everyone the freedom to choose whether or not they are drawn to practice a religion. One who does not feel comfortable practicing an organized religion does not deserve to be looked down upon by those who do.

There are people who are very religious who break the laws of human decency, and there are people who do not feel comfortable choosing a religion for themselves who nonetheless are moral, ethical and admirable. Do not be quick to judge one of those who are following their inner compass but going in a different direction than you think they should be going. It is up to each person to determine what nurtures his or her inner growth and spirituality.

I placed within each person a longing to merge back into Myself. That is what you are feeling when you are bothered by feelings of disconnectedness within yourself. When your life is calm, and everything seems to be going okay, but you have an inner sense of disenfranchisement, you are longing to feel your connectedness with Me. Everyone came forth from Me and will eventually return to Me.

I am One with each of you individually. When you feel disconnected from Me, do something about it! Find a quiet place where you can be alone and stop the swirl of thoughts, fears or problems that may be churning through your conscious mind.

Call out to Me within your mind. Then remain still and try to detect a sign from Me. Do not discount the chirping of a bird as being a response from Me or a delicate feeling of peacefulness wafting over you. I can respond in any number of ways to a call from one of My beloveds.

As important as it is for you to know without a doubt that you are beloved to me, it is of equal importance for you to clearly grasp that every other person is profoundly cherished by Me as well. I would like for all of you to value each other as I hold dear each of you. Do not allow different beliefs or interpretations to put a wedge between you and others.

Be fluid, instead of rigid, with your expectations. Graciously accept the preferences of others. There is no one human model for all to follow. I have told you before that I enjoy the differences and variety of characteristics that you each express. I want you to be your unique self.

Religions have the potential to lead people straight to Me. Unfortunately, religions can also act as a divider to cast aside certain people and create misfortune for them. I implore you to use respect and common sense and not to interfere with another person's freedom to choose their spiritual expression for themself. Each person deserves to have the freedom to make the choice of his or her own spiritual expression without pressure from family members or anyone else who might be all too willing to pass a negative judgment on their decision.

There are two critically important decisions for a person to make during their life. The first that I will mention is the decision to be true to one's self, to have the self-respect and the inner strength to forge one's own path even when it may seem to be unorthodox or unappealing to others. You cannot comfortably walk in shoes that do not fit you properly, and you cannot comfortably march to a different tune than the one that reverberates within you.

The second critically important decision is to honor yourself in all that you do and be certain that all that you do is honorable. Even when you are not conforming to the more common ways to be, relax and be yourself. Do not be afraid to express yourself as you naturally are, and do not look askance when others express their uniqueness. All are My children, and all deserve the freedom to express themselves as they naturally are.

Quite a large number of people assess themselves as a model person holding their heads up high with the judgment that others should be as they are. Humanity has too much self-elevation and not enough other-elevation especially when the other person differs greatly from one's self. Some people only know their look-a-likes as being valuable and discount the rest. Human nature, you may say. I say this must change. The need to glorify one's self is a sign of weakness and insecurity. It is also a sign of narrow-mindedness.

When people think mainly of themselves and especially treasure those who fit their personal model, they are either delusional or ignorant and often both. All too often, a lack of respect is dished out to those who do not look like or hold the same values as oneself. Can you not see how restrictive this is? Can you imagine there being only one flavor of ice cream? What if only eating one kind of fruit was acceptable? What if everyone was required to ignore all the other wonderful fruit and eat only bananas to make themselves acceptable to other people?

It is important to discern the higher road in life and to take that road. Notice how many choices you make every day and recognize which are beneficial to your evolutionary development and those that are not. Target for elimination those that are not raising you up to a higher standard of self-expression. Keep in mind that part of ethical conduct is to value all of humanity and to make a special effort to branch away from only including those who are mainly like yourself as being the most worthwhile. Broaden your horizons, and do not only eat bananas every day.

When people judge their religious preference as being elevated above the preferences of others and then put their noses in the air and become arrogant, they are only shopping at one store. Whenever someone opens their heart to Me, I reach back to them, and it does not matter if they are in a synagogue, a mosque or in the peace and quiet of their own backyard. If you want to follow the religion you learned as a child, if it truly fulfills you, then continue along in your family's tradition, but do not be loath to investigate other forms of worship than what you were introduced to as a child. Different styles of shoes fit different forms of feet. Find a good fit for yourself and be comfortable drawing close to Me in whichever way is most fulfilling for you.

I will tell you what pleases Me very much. I am delighted when a person sets their mind to reaching Me directly. Sometimes following religious customs can actually put a barrier between us. Do you like someone talking to you so much that you cannot get a word in edgewise? Reach for Me within the silence. I like when people go deeply within themselves into the peace and stillness that resides at the center of their being, turning off all of the distractions of the outer world. This sets the stage for them to draw close to Me.

I am within every one of you, but you usually ignore My presence because you are so involved in the outer world. Your physicality makes it difficult for you to sense another level of your being. I do not beat drums or toot horns to get your attention. You have to find Me patiently waiting for you within your heart. That is where I reside.

I reside in the part of you, which pours out love. Love is My nature, and it is your nature as well. I let My nature show, and I want all of you to resonate with what I am telling you and to bring out the pure love that resides within your hearts.

Develop your spiritual life, and you will enjoy the expansion of life satisfaction. Your spiritual life and your physical life are inseparable. Your physical life usually dominates your attention, and it is easy to ignore your spiritual life with all of your physical life's activities and demands.

Look at your life and think about what is important to you right now, and then think about ten or twenty years from now. Will your life's priorities be the same? Life's priorities point you in the direction that is most necessary to pay attention to at that particular time. Make room for Me in your life and make developing closeness with Me your enduring top priority.

My children, come to Me personally and spend time with just Me. If you close your eyes to the outer world and search for Me within your inner world, I will pull you close to Me. Here is a quick instruction.

> Become mentally settled, peaceful and quiet. Close your eyes and hold as your intention being receptive to feeling My presence within you. Be calm and open-minded. Then gently repeat within your mind, "Creator God, come to me so I can feel you."

You will be creating closeness with Me that sooner or later will result in a light tingling sensation flowing through your body. This is the signal of My presence beginning to expand within you.

This method will not work when your mind is cluttered with life's problems and desires. They are what holds you to the delusion that we are separate from each other. This delusion has been keeping your civilization from advancing. Erase this delusion.

> Now I invite you to take a giant step towards manifesting yourself as an enlightened person. Read, reread and study the teachings I am giving you and conscientiously work with them. Become more advanced in your self-expression. Begin with accepting all others as your dear sisters and brothers and extend your respect and protection. Hold reverence for all people regardless of how you may have felt about some of them in the past.

As I embrace all of you, I want you to embrace each other and to open the doors you may have closed to caring about certain others. If you love Me, start seeing all other people as parts of Myself. When you see people, who are strangers to you, send them thought messages such as, "I love you. I love you. We are family." As you see people on the street, mentally say to yourself, "There goes my sister. There goes my brother." Deliberately send forth your love towards those who may have seemed offensive to you in some way.

If you are driving a car and you stop for a red light, do not waste this valuable time. Look around and send love from your heart to all those you see. Open your heart wide and become My representative who is dedicated to holding all people within his or her heart.

CHAPTER FIFTEEN

PROTECTING YOUR PLANET

———

When you honor and revere the preciousness of all people, you are a delight to Me, and you will become a delight to yourself as well. Use this as the cornerstone of your life, and know that I am smiling upon you whenever you value all people. Every time you acknowledge the preciousness of every person in your heart, you are ringing My doorbell. I want every person on Earth to ring My doorbell in unison.

The most common error that humanity makes is thinking that they only live once and the way they are during their current lifetime is their one true self. In fact, humanity repeatedly returns, each time playing a different role. The pauper becomes the prince. The rich man becomes the laborer. What usually stays the same is that the hero from one lifetime typically becomes a hero in their next lifetime as well.

Those who develop the urge to help people find that same characteristic showing up repeatedly. Those who were a strong positive force for good during their physical life often feel compelled to return to Earth to help humanity evolve. Many of these people had inglorious endings to some of their previous lifetimes when they stood out from the crowd for their compassion and their humanitarian instincts.

You might want to evaluate your life at this point, particularly for evidence of strong traits you have that either do not fall into the category of being beneficial and worth carrying back with you the next time you experience an earthly incarnation or are just the opposite. Look for the traits of being kind-hearted and compassionate, patient and understanding, eager to assist and doing more than is necessary, and above all, accepting every other person as your equal and you as theirs. This is the winning formula to bring about a worldwide evolutionary leap forward that your world clearly needs to initiate.

I am evaluating the chances of all the people on Earth pulling together to get along with each other far better than they have been and whether your Earth will be patient a while longer to give your populations an opportunity to swiftly advance their efforts to cleanse and purify her land masses and oceans. It is almost too late to prevent the Earth from giving up on humanity's shortsighted foolishness. You will be crying in the decades to come with deep sorrow over the condition of your planet.

You will be crying over the lives that become lost due to the snap-back experienced worldwide by an enraged planet who moves to throw humanity off her surface. These are not idle words. You and your younger generations are going to take the brunt of insufficient food that is safe enough to eat and water that is pure enough to drink. Life will be enormously challenging.

> I am not exaggerating, so do not foolishly discount what I am saying. If you love your planet, take action now and press forward to repair the damage already inflicted upon her before she roars back at you.

You resist acting rationally, refusing to take responsibility for what you are creating because you think that you will be long gone when the problems become insurmountable. I have news for you who hold this misperception. Environmental problems are close to being insurmountable already while you refuse to recognize their present and future impact on humanity. A horror show on Earth is in the making, caused by negligence, which discounts the importance of restoring Earth's original state.

Humanity is turning from honoring and protecting the land to neglecting the land. The American Indians venerated the land, which they held close to their hearts. Now it is common to discount the preciousness of clear lakes and waterways and unadulterated soil. These are only some of the insults humanity is directing to your planet's well-being.

Using formerly pristine oceans as dumping grounds introduces toxicity into the food supply derived from the oceans, limiting humanity's ability to maintain their health and well-being when they consume food sourced from the oceans. Pristine sources of air to breathe, food to eat and water to drink are disappearing due to the influence of businesses, which hold their profit margins as being more important than the purity of the land and people's ability to maintain strong, healthy bodies. In the not distant future, humanity will regret having taken the fool's way out.

Every day Earth's populations add to these problems, which already are too burdensome for your planet to overcome. Your dallying when committed action is required sets your planet even further behind in its struggle to overcome human negligence. You do not stand tall to honor and protect your planet. You do not put your will and your energy into preserving the viability of your planet, while you take full advantage of what is available in the moment, with no sense of responsibility for what tomorrow brings.

Wake up to the dangerous situation that is enveloping your precious planet Earth, and demonstrate your love and respect for her. It may not be too late if every person takes action to halt the advanced putrefaction of your planet. Do not think of your planet as an inanimate object. She is a creation of Mine, just as each of you is a creation of Mine. Do you not want respect and protection from harm? This is what she wants, and up until now, she has been extraordinarily patient and forgiving. The jig is up. She is not going to continue to tolerate ill-treatment without making a fuss.

This is what is most likely to happen. There will not be enough people or governments willing to extend themselves to clean up the environment. Most will not step forward to preserve the integrity of Earth's atmosphere by turning away from utilizing fossil fuels as an energy source. Many businesses will continue to employ fossil fuel usage for the monetary payoff. By the time they wise up to the suffocating conditions they have brought down upon humanity, it will be too late to undo the environmental disaster that they fostered.

Each of you knows how much easier it is to recognize a problem in the making and take steps to avert it ahead of time than to look back and realize that every sign of the problem was evident, but you did nothing to resolve it before it erupted into a nightmare. You have a nightmare brewing right under your noses. Few people understand the extent of the consequences that will arise from humanity's negligence.

Your planet Earth has the same requirements that your physical body has. Your body requires fresh air to breathe and clean water to drink. If you put a person into a chamber and only supply that chamber with dirty water and air that is unsafe to breathe, the person will sicken and die unless they take charge of their situation and, somehow or another, find a way to blast themselves out of that chamber. Consider yourselves expendable as far as your planet is concerned. She is going to take action to safeguard herself, so do not expect her to put your safety and convenience above her own.

I am telling you this before it is too late to undo the damage already done and to give you the chance to take aggressive action to safeguard your planet Earth. Do not continue to turn away from the responsibility that you all share. If you are a resident of planet Earth, you have a stake in her health and well-being.

You do not trash your valuables. You treasure and care for them. So why are you allowing the treasure, which is your planet Earth, to become dirtied, over-populated and denigrated by lack of respect and caring for her? I object to your lazy dismissal of the extreme necessity to do everything within your power to forestall the inevitable disaster in the making for every one of you.

I am warning you that if you continue to delay taking collective steps, fully supported by nearly everyone on Earth, you will greatly suffer when it is too late to reverse extremely negative conditions for most of Earth's inhabitants. How much clearer can I get? You, who discount the necessity to safeguard the well-being of your planet, will be castigating yourselves mightily as you struggle with fear and regret. Your planet will not be pleasant or accommodating anymore. She will be violent and merciless, and she will not care what she brings down upon humanity.

> You are headed for disaster by not joining together to do everything that is within your power to organize a unified response to climate change and all the threats to human health and well-being that come from using your planet as a garbage can. I urge you to be practical and act swiftly.

You must generate commitment from people who disregard the urgency to take action. You must change those people's minds and gain their support. Those who understand the urgency for unified action are waiting for effective leadership to present a guide for protecting your planet and your safety. The time for being dumb and lazy is over. You all need to smarten up and get to work.

I do not know how to jolt you into action other than to tell you what life will be like in the not-too-distant future if you continue to dismiss the need for a universal joint effort to protect your planet's viability as a residential home for human beings. For most of the world, your markets accommodate shoppers with choices of foodstuffs that are healthy for you to eat. In the future, there will be shortages, and the foods that you rely on will be unavailable or no longer healthy for you to consume.

If you depend upon food sources from your oceans, you will be disappointed because many of them will be no longer be edible. You will be hungry. And, the typical diet that you have been accustomed to eating will no longer be safe for you to consume.

Rain will fall irregularly, and droughts will become more and more common. Extremely high temperatures and extremely low temperatures will replace traditional weather patterns. It will be as if your planet is off-kilter and trying to disrupt humanity's peace of mind. Crops will fail. Weeds and insects will flourish, and food sources from waterways will be unsafe to consume.

If this does not sound severe, think about how you feel when the food that you are used to eating is not available, and you must substitute unappealing alternatives. Think about how it will feel to go to bed hungry when there is not enough food to eat. Conditions upon your planet will deteriorate extensively and cause disruptions in nutrition, housing and medical care for masses of people greatly affected by Earth's tumultuous upheavals.

The worst part of the deterioration of living conditions upon your planet is that an obvious downward trajectory of living conditions will take hold. As it is now, if you all pulled together to clean your waterways, your atmosphere, and you took steps to end your habitual misuse and abuse of your land masses, you can envision your planet becoming better equipped to continue to support humanity's presence. If you wait too long to begin amelioration of previous damage done, the task will be too overwhelming to achieve. You as a species will pay a high price for your reluctance to move decisively to safeguard your planet from humanity's disrespect and negligence.

Forward thinkers do not have a very good record of persuading complacent others to overcome their innate resistance to change; change that is required, but to the complacent just seems to be an inconvenience. Taking the higher road in life requires one to put up with inconveniences at times. The lazy way forward creates a price to pay later.

This is where your planet stands now. There are dire consequences if humanity, as a whole, does not undertake full responsibility for the cleansing of the land, the water and the air to the greatest extent possible, as soon as possible.

> To cleanse your planet, some businesses will have to hold the condition of the Earth above their push to make more money. Purifying the Earth will require determination and high moral integrity from everyone, including those who have been acting without integrity as they dump waste into the environment.

Those industries and businesses that introduce carbon emissions into the atmosphere and refuse to acknowledge the overriding benefits of solar power are behaving foolishly. It will be their descendants as well as the rest of humanity who will breathe poisons into their lungs. The sins of the fathers come home to roost in their descendants.

Respect your land, the air and the water if you want humanity to thrive. Clean up your planet and do not heap more distress upon her natural state of being. Hold your planet close to your heart, and treat it with the greatest care and respect, if you want her to continue to support your residence upon her surface. I am alerting you that you are treading on thin ice as you continue to ignore the warnings of environmentalists who have the Earth's well-being in mind.

With unlimited population increases, human life on Earth has been heading toward becoming unsustainable. Your planet simply cannot continue to supply your species with adequate resources to guarantee the health and well-being of significantly increasing populations, which are casting off catastrophic amounts of refuse and polluting the waterways. Your oceans have cradled life on Earth from the beginning, and your populations seem intent on making the oceans so sickly that the food resources that the oceans have been providing will no longer be available to you. What will happen when masses of hungry people eat fish from polluted waters, fish that will sicken them? You may think that the oceans will always provide for you, but I am telling you, this is very shortsighted.

You treat your landmasses as poorly as you treat your oceans. Until recent times, there was plenty of land to raise livestock and plant sufficient crops to supply your populations. This is no longer the case. In a large part of the world, populations have expanded exponentially. There are many more mouths to feed, and often the food they have to eat is insufficient.

In some countries, it has become an accepted practice to add unnatural chemical compounds to the soil in order to increase yields. Although some of these chemicals are not supportive to human bodies, they are financially supportive to the companies that manufacture those compounds. Humanity is at a crossroads between choosing moral, ethical behavior or continuing to line business' pockets at the expense of people's health and well-being.

If Earth had two-thirds of the population that it currently does, and solar power replaced burning fossil fuels as your energy source, humanity's stay on Earth would be limitless. As it is now, with the stresses of overpopulation plus the deterioration of the quality of the air and other factors, you are living on borrowed time.

Now I want you to consider how some of your religions have discouraged methods of birth control and how many people follow the dictates of these religions. Mindlessly following a religion's precepts that are irrational is not the fault of the religion as much as their followers' propensity to follow irrational rules. Throughout time, human sexuality has been misjudged by some religions in particular, who used their authority to regulate and cast a dirty spell upon a God-given gift to humanity.

Dirtiness is in the eye of the beholder, and those who see dirtiness in the loving drawing together of people who truly hold each other dear and deeply care for one another are not worthy of speaking for Me. Too much credibility has been given to those who purport to speak in My name. From their misconstrued perceptions of My will have arisen wrong dictates, as well as intolerable injustices doled out to innocents.

I have already stated that My gift of sexuality has many expressions. I will also state that My gift of sexuality has been misunderstood and abused by those who attempt to regulate, judge and demean its expression.

Any form of sexual expression that does not honor and protect the well-being of those who participate is abhorrent, and I do not want My children hurting each other in any way. I also do not want My children bringing harm to their planet and themselves by producing more children than their planet can accommodate. Protect the populations that already exist by using precaution to prevent insemination, such as birth control methods that are scientifically proven effective and safe for long-term use.

The urge to reproduce is strong, yet at this time in humanity's history, a lowered birth rate will be supportive to your planet and to humanity's ability to continue to reside upon her surface.

Everything I have said to you is rational. What is not rational is going forward as you have been, making the same kinds of decisions that are undermining the ability of your planet to continue providing for her populations as she has in the past. With every polluting choice you make, you make it harder for you in the years ahead when the pollution worsens and your bodies reflect the impurities they have ingested.

The decisions that you make now will determine your ability to survive upon Earth in the future and the future I am talking about is not far off. Already you are affected. You are just not cognizant that you are.

When your religions tell you that they speak for Me, and what they say is not rational, tread lightly and remain skeptical. There is no one religion that speaks for Me. Most religions still carry beliefs and practices that reflect the times in which they were founded.

When plagues and famines wiped out vast numbers of people, there was a legitimate need to boost the populations. Now the opposite is occurring. The legitimate need is for a reduction in population growth to accommodate the very real and not imagined disastrous situation that is advancing upon Earth.

Polluted oceans mean seafood that is unfit to eat. Eating unsafe seafood introduces toxins into one's body, which interfere with your body's ability to heal itself when you become sick and makes it less likely that you will live to a ripe old age. In addition, if you do live to old age, you will be far less comfortable than you would have been had you safeguarded your food supply. When a person is in their youth, it may not seem to slow them down as much if their diet lacks solid, good nutrition, but as people age, their bodies become less able to recover when their nutritional levels are substandard. All throughout people's lives, they will be more likely to thrive physically when the purity of the food supply does not undermine their well-being.

Having too many people on Earth is a recipe for catastrophe. Pollution, overpopulation, and taking a wait-and-see attitude instead of taking charge of coming up with broad-based initiatives and implementing them worldwide will escalate the challenges that the human race is creating for itself. You may pray to Me to help you overcome these problems, which I am already doing by educating you firsthand through this direct communication.

You have created this unsafe situation on Earth, and it is your responsibility to fix it. I am not going to coddle you and make things better. You are going to sink or swim together, so you had better learn to work cooperatively with a shared determination to reverse the putrefying of your planet and to assume strict reproductive responsibility.

There have been warnings, which people broadly disregard. Accept this communication from Me as your last warning and know that if you disregard this notification and go along as you have been, you will be filled with regret, deep regret, that you failed to take action when you should have. Do not leave it up to someone else to lead the way. Every single person needs to become involved to make every contribution that they can to preserve the health and well-being of your planet. This does not mean that I do not love you, but it does mean that it is time for the human race to grow up and take responsibility for preserving the gift they have been given.

Do not discount what I am saying to you. Get to work immediately. I am tired of allowing you to evolve at your own rate and be satisfied, thinking that there is not much you can do to ensure the safety and protection of your planetary home. Consider this your wake-up call.

Rethink your predilection to hold back when the soundness of your planetary home faces threat after threat, while most of you do nothing to halt humanity's negligence. You must stop sitting on your hands with your eyes closed. Wake up to your responsibility to safeguard human life and the planet that gives you the opportunity to return repeatedly, enjoying her tremendous beauty while you slowly evolve yourselves.

It is going to take all of you dedicating yourself to protecting the Earth to ensure that Earth continues to remain a viable residence. There will be more signs from your planetary home that she is getting restless and more and more displeased by humanity's lack of protection. Be watchful of the warning signs, which will be numerous. You can discount them and carry on as you have been, but if you do, there will be consequences, and they will be unpleasant for nearly everyone on Earth.

If you want to prevent the unpleasant deterioration of the quality of life on Earth, do not waste a day. Get busy reforming your deficient attitudes and behaviors immediately. It is your responsibility to do everything within your power to ensure humanity's ability to continue to inhabit your planet. I want to point out that everyone needs to progress along this path. Those who do not will pull down the efforts of the rest, and this is not advisable.

Dangerous situations are brewing. Your planet is overpopulated. The land in many places and the oceans are losing their purity. Any sane, thoughtful person sees what is happening, and yet there is not a major push to deal with the ever-expanding problems ahead for humanity.

This communication is a wake-up call for every person on Earth. The longer you wait, telling yourself that you will think about what I am espousing without taking immediate action, the more you will delay the positive effect that you can contribute. Taking corrective action to right the wrongs in human perceptions and behavior needed to be in effect for a long time already. So far, humanity has mostly been lazy and self-centered. Rather than remaining this way, all people need to become judicious and practical regarding the protection of your planet.

Given the lack of cooperation and discord that is raging upon your planet, I do not have the conviction that enough can be done soon enough to forestall massive misfortune hitting you where it will hurt. Do not shrug your shoulders and think to yourself, "Ah, nothing unusual is going to happen." I am going to begin very soon to unleash your planet's fury over her maltreatment.

Heed My warning. The human race is going to have more to deal with than their current problems. Landmasses will begin to shift as if on a timer that I have set. There will be disturbing loss of life close to shorelines, and this will be an indicator of what is going to happen inland as well. I am telling you not to ignore My warnings, for the longer you delay taking unified action, the more violently your planet will express her outrage.

If humanity as a whole set out to follow My instructions and adopt My standards, something wonderful would happen. The dire rumblings of the Earth would diminish, and loss of life would become forestalled. Do not think that there is any other way to straighten out the human race than to bring consequences for their unenlightened treatment of each other and their beloved planet. Too many people have their heads in the sand. They have turned off the switch of rationality within their minds.

Everything I have said to you is rational. Anyone can see the deterioration of the formerly pristine environment on Earth. That humanity cannot get along with each other is patently obvious. Rich people pile up their fortunes while mostly ignoring the needs of the masses. Often, their hearts have shrunken as their pocketbooks have expanded.

Many changes are about to take place on Earth. The direction that the changes take is up to you as a species. If you heed My warnings and follow the directions that I am giving, you will enter a time that will bring you a lot of pleasure. If you do not heed My warnings, you will enter a time of ever-increasing chaos and destruction, which will swallow up huge land masses along with the people that were living upon them.

CHAPTER SIXTEEN

YOUR EVOLUTIONARY DEVELOPMENT

———

My precious children, take My advice and run towards embracing everything that is good and supportive for your planet and eschew all things that are not. Find partners who are willing to undertake the enormous environmental cleanup that must occur. Everyone must participate. You must be willing to put up with discomfort in the short term to gain long-term security for your species to remain on this planet under humane living conditions.

I am not going to continue to stay on the sidelines only as an observer while humanity continues to make little progress in catching on to exactly what constitutes rational, decent behavior towards each other and towards your planetary residence. You are travelers through space and time whose main objective is to refine yourselves to become as I am. However, you continue being confused, even about what you are seeing with your own two eyes.

Most of you may as well be blind, deaf and dumb. You do not see the obvious. You are deaf to warnings extended by experts who clearly understand the deterioration of your planet's ability to house expanding populations. You are dumb to think that you can continue to go along as you have been and everything will be all right.

I am speaking out to spur you, as a species, into action to set a deliberate course for yourselves, which will halt the deterioration of your health and well-being in absolute synchronization with halting your planet's deterioration of its health and well-being.

If you think that you will live healthy, happy lives while your planet becomes more and more overrun with your unenlightened behavior, you are naïve. It is nearly too late to introduce enough broad-based improvements to halt the deterioration of your planetary home and for people everywhere to pull together cooperatively to address environmental protection. Your species cannot even get along with each other, much less pull together in common cause to prevent a catastrophic situation upon your planet.

Part of the problem is the naysayers who do not comprehend that which they will not allow themselves to see. They are blindly trusting that all these problems are exaggerated and will resolve themselves. Do you detect a magical resolution of environmental deterioration?

When your house gets dirty, does it magically clean itself? When your body gets stinky, does the odor magically go away? Who is responsible for the condition of your body, your house and your planet? My dear children, each of you is responsible for restoring your planet to its pristine state, and My suggestion is for you to stop pulling against the obvious reality that your planet is endangered if she does not act to protect herself.

You may think of your planet Earth as an object that just exists. If you hold this perception, you are mistaken. All of the planets, the suns and the moons, the rivers, ponds and oceans are all part of Myself. All have My essence as their being, just as you do.

For Me, it is like it is for you. Your hands are important to you, and you want them to remain in good condition, or you are unhappy. The same goes for your heart and your liver, and your other body parts. Your body consists of all of its parts, and if one part does not work properly, discomfort results. If you were Me, you would feel every stress and strain that humanity brings upon the landmasses, the atmosphere on Earth and the waterways. You would personally detect within the essence of yourself all the problems that Earth is putting up with due to humanity's malfeasance.

If all of you naysayers, who refuse to accept the validity of concerns about the continuing viability of your planet Earth, could feel what I am feeling from your Earth's discomfort, you would do everything within your power to restore Earth's pristine condition. Your arguments against taking responsibility for Earth's deteriorating condition smack of laziness and stupidity. You will wise up in the future when there is no getting around acknowledging the destruction that humanity has imposed upon her host planet.

If you naysayers refuse to act swiftly and cooperatively with the rest of humanity, I will have no other option than to allow Mother Earth to roar back at you. When she begins to roar, you will wish that you could turn back the hands of time to have another chance to take her needs seriously.

> You must stop thinking of your planet as an inanimate object. She has consciousness just as you do, but she is far more responsible than you are. She has delayed bringing about wholesale destruction. She has been patient, giving out some warnings but withholding massive violence until all hope is lost for humanity to take full responsibility for Earth's well-being.

I am not going to keep her from deciding to act against humanity's residence upon her surface. I am going to allow her to protect herself. I have almost given up any hope that humanity will pull together and behave responsibly toward their planet and toward the rest of humanity.

Humanity as a whole does not reflect My values, My compassion or My work ethic. If cleaning up your planet seems like too great a task to perform, then you do nothing, or very little, to provide for its restitution. Just when every single person should sign on to participate in the enormous task ahead, people do very little and mostly take a wait-and-see stance.

You behave like young children who rely on mom and dad to take care of you. The problem is that children have to grow up and become responsible for themselves. Very few of you have undertaken the responsibility to ensure the continuation of your residence upon your planet. I warn humanity that you are already seeing signs of her striking back, and these signs will grow stronger and be more devastating. Stand up and make the important decisions and the tough choices, which will restore Earth's pristine nature before you poison your Earth to a greater and greater extent.

I am doing My best to drive home the fact that your future is going to be bleak if there is not a tremendous unified effort to restore your planet's pristine nature. This can be done but, certain industries will object and probably none more than the petroleum industry. Burning fossil fuels is one of the most dangerous and expendable activities that needs to be immediately phased out.

Use technology to utilize energy from renewable sources such as solar power and wind power to replace your reliance on fossil fuels. The question you have to ask yourselves is, should humanity's ability to reside upon this planet take precedence over allowing the fossil fuel companies to continue to make money for a while longer?

This should be the first step: eliminate all fossil fuel usage and substitute solar, wind and other natural environmental sources of power. The second step should be to institute universal shipping standards that safeguard the oceans and waterways.

People prefer to hold on to what they have, and they can find all kinds of ways to justify turning away from protecting their environment. Do not be flexible when it comes to environmental protections. Insist that under all circumstances, you will not allow any form of polluting of your land, air or waterways, not even a minor amount.

So-called minor amounts add up over time and diminish the pristine nature of the water as it was before humanity discounted the importance of water quality for the sake of commerce. You will notice that as humanity became more involved in commerce, they became less respectful of the natural environment. Too often, it comes down to getting more for oneself rather than respecting and preserving what one already has. Having all the money in the world will not make up for having to drink impure water or having to breathe poisonous air.

People's ambitions and goals may create more havoc than satisfaction. There is great satisfaction in getting ahead in life, earning more money and being successful. That immediate fulfillment lingers as long as nothing interferes.

The challenge comes when unforeseen problems arise, and a person has to choose between losing some of their income to take the higher road in life, or ignore the higher road to accept an inferior decision that exposes the environment to significant damage. People and businesses who pollute the atmosphere, the land and the waters without considering the long-term effects are stealing the future of humanity. They are lessening the likelihood that humanity will continue its long-term residence upon your planet.

I am telling you and the rest of humanity that you cannot go on as you have been, disrespecting that which you depend on to maintain your health and well-being.

Look beyond your noses and think about what your planet requires to maintain her viability. Then set out with a determined joint effort to deliver all that she requires to continue to sustain life upon her surface without sacrificing her well-being.

This may sound like a script for a science fiction movie, but it will be all too real for those of you who are alive when the cataclysms begin. Imagine news stories describing the massive loss of life due to more and more frequent volcanic eruptions, violent earthquakes, flooding, and vast areas suffering from arid droughts. You will experience the worst that the Earth has to offer but not spread out over vast expanses of time. It will be as if a destructive orchestra is playing its funeral dirge for humanity.

Do not shrug your shoulders and let what I say go by without stopping to envision how this would affect you and your loved ones. Most people have been in a state of denial since the first red flags raised to alert the world community of the warming weather patterns, the melting of the glaciers and the displacement of animal life from their natural cold weather habitats. Unfortunately, not enough people are inclined to be seriously concerned about global warming as long as their iceberg has not melted.

Your early forecasters received the cold shoulder of disbelief when they beat the drum of danger lying ahead because of the over-heating of your planet. People were curious about what the forecasters had to say, but they viewed the warnings as conjecture even as scientific evidence proved otherwise. Those who were perceptive enough to read the scientific research and interpret it accurately could not awaken broad-scale concern among the general population.

People allowed the time of opportunity when the problems were less than they are now to go by without recognizing how those problems would mushroom into catastrophic proportions. Most people have no idea of the amount of deterioration that has gone on within the Earth's atmosphere from carbon dioxide emissions and other greenhouse gases. Concern for the environment gets in the way of business and moneymaking, which come first for those who hold monetary gain as a higher priority than the long-term safety of their planet and their planet's populations.

You are making your planet uninhabitable. I am not telling you that in a thousand years your planet will be uninhabitable. You are in the midst of your planet becoming uninhabitable right now. There is no organized cooperative effort to convince people everywhere to join together to follow well-constructed, effective guidelines for taking destructive pressure off of Earth as quickly and efficiently as possible. Every person, every business and every country's government needs to come into line to support Earth-healthy practices, which are clearly specified by scientists who have studied the Earth's condition and know exactly what needs to be done to reverse the damage continually being inflicted upon her.

What do you think the chances are that all people, all businesses and all governments will embrace that which I recommend? Hoping and wishing do not count. Very few people are willing to cut back and sacrifice today for the extended benefits that would accrue to future generations and the glorious planet upon which you live.

Your planet is not a fool. She knows who is causing her unhealthy state. She has the capacity to protect herself, and in a very short time, you will witness the vehemence of your planet moving you off her surface.

In a series of maneuvers, which your planet is fully capable of implementing, she will express her rage at humanity's gross negligence of her health and safety. I have warned you before that she cannot continue to support ever-increasing populations, which disrespect her need to maintain her own health and well-being. If someone mistreats you, do you decide to do all you can to help him or her?

Your planet is going to send most of humanity packing. In a rage and with fury, she will roar over and over and be extreme in her violence towards the populations who take her for granted and do not care for her in return for all she has provided. Catastrophic events will occur with regularity. Humanity will be grief-stricken and regret that they dismissed her needs while they focused primarily on their own self-centeredness. This is what humanity is setting in motion by continuing its deleterious impact on their planetary home.

After she rejects most of humanity from remaining upon her surface, the Earth will take time to repair herself, and during this time, she will only house a very small number of human beings. These people will mainly be those who feel greatly attached to her in a deeply loving, caring, respectful way. These people will get along well, and because there will be so few of them, your planet Earth will regain her pristine nature once again. You must face the probability that you and your descendants will no longer be welcome to live upon Earth.

Instead of dying and then being reborn on Earth to continue your evolutionary progress, you will be reborn in another location where you will continue to evolve. I am not going to transfer you to a more advanced planet because your populations would be likely to disrupt their evolutionary progress. I will relocate you to a planet similar to Earth, which your scientists have not yet discovered because it is in a slightly higher vibrational frequency than Earth. Hence, it is not perceivable to people on Earth.

Your scientists have not unveiled the secrets of My creation as much as they think they have. There is far more to My creation than their instrumentation can discern. They do not take into consideration the rate of vibration, which determines visibility to those who are acclimated to the third-dimensional sphere of existence. The third-dimensional vibrational rate is lower than the vibrational rates within the higher spheres of existence. The person who is receiving My dictation for this educational communication is unable to discern a form speaking to her, and yet she detects My vibration and hears the words that I am speaking.

She demonstrates evidence of linking with My intelligence as she records My dictation. You are used to the physical world and its barriers, which seem clearly defined. Earth has the lowest vibrational rate of all of the planetary bodies, making it nearly impossible to breach the invisible vibrational barrier that keeps people on Earth from seeing and interacting with higher vibrational existences. This is a deliberate part of My plan. I isolate humanity from negatively interfering with more evolved societies on other planes of existence.

You may feel that you are the only inhabitants of My creation because you cannot detect any others. That is not nearly enough proof for you to go on. Do not look around and presume that you have the full picture. Only those, who have scaled the heights of evolutionary development, know the full picture.

All of the rest of you are striving to equal their evolutionary progress, although you are not cognizant that this is the goal of your existence. Why do you think that you are alive on Earth? Have you ever pondered the answer to this question?

Hardly anyone alive on Earth thinks about such matters. Most are thinking that for some unknown reason, they exist, be it for only one lifetime, and then they let it go at that. Very few seek to determine the meaning of life or the meaning of their existence. They enjoy today and do not give much thought to the *why* of it all. Why are they here living on Earth, and what is going on that they are not grasping?

Very few question to that extent. Of all of your populations, less than one percent are determined to reach an enlightened state of being before they pass from their bodies. If you do not set a course for yourself, you are not likely to arrive at the most preferable destination.

Most people float through life doing what they have to do to take care of themselves and their dependents and pay very little attention to their evolutionary progress.

Improving one's morals and ethics are rarely one's life ambition. Being charitable or kind to others is more a product of past conditioning rather than of deliberately choosing to instill these admirable traits within oneself.

When people are satisfied to remain as they naturally have been and do not determine to push themselves to develop more admirable traits and behaviors, they stagnate. Life becomes boring, and they go looking for more of an undefinable something to make them feel satisfied. People waste their lives when they bob along without a plan to evolve themselves.

I highly recommend that you recognize how you have been without glossing over your lesser qualities. Most people would relish pointing out someone else's lesser aspects while ignoring their own. I suggest that you focus on your own delinquent traits with a determination to modify them in a good way. Do not expect them to transform without a focused effort, and be sure to congratulate yourself when positive behavioral modifications begin to appear. It is important for you to notice your improvement.

> I want you to step into the conscious side of life. Become consciously self-aware and self-correcting. Then you will feel good about yourself, and it will not be for frivolous reasons. I am defining what you need to know in order to take a big step up the evolutionary ladder and be securely on your way to expressing yourself as a child of Mine.

As I have said repeatedly, every one of you is My offspring, and I love you unconditionally. I do not want you to suffer, and I do not want you to delay your inevitable realization that you can be as I am. I always want the best for all of My children, but I require that they progress upon their evolutionary path at a quicker pace than they have been.

I admit that I am pushing you along now and that I have not been putting pressure on you before now. You see, you would not pay much attention to what I am telling you if you were confident that you and your world were safe and secure and that life is a picnic. If you felt that life was a picnic before this time in Earth's history, I suspect that you do not hold that same perception anymore.

If you maintain sensitivity to the suffering of other people, you have been in pain and despair watching world events unfold and witnessing the harshness brought to bear upon so many innocent people.

I am holding all of you responsible for expanding your humanitarian efforts. Put your arms around those who require assistance. Some countries resist accepting people who are destitute and may have brought some problem makers with them. I understand these concerns, but I am asking you to extend assistance as best that you can, as groups and individuals, to give displaced or impoverished people a much-needed fresh start in life.

Always picture in your mind how you would feel if you were in their situation, and then do not hold back assistance that you are capable of extending. If you are not there in person to extend aid, find a way to send financial support through charities and organizations that are determined to help them.

I need people on Earth to act for Me. I need warm-hearted compassionate people to take care of My precious children, your sisters and brothers. Have a big open heart for all but most especially for those who are in desperate situations.

Sometimes one person alone can bring miraculous grace to another person's life. Only if you extend yourself will you have that blessed opportunity. To give is to receive, and to have the means to give should propel you forward with vigor and determination to share your excess open-heartedly and then feel enormous satisfaction within yourself.

I implore you not to sit on your excess assets, which do nothing for you other than supporting your ego. Abandon the need to have more in favor of doing more for the many people who are in desperate situations. Be open and gracious with your assistance, and know that I am personally grateful to you for responding to My plea to put loving arms around people who have desperate needs.

I value every one of you. I never release anyone from My heart, even though many of you have assumed that I do. I am patient and understanding, and I know right from wrong, which many of you have trouble discerning. I work through some of you who feel My ever-expanding love for all people.

I want to give all of you the opportunity to feel My presence within yourself and to act for Me within your physical world to take care of My children who are having a hard time with their lives. Do not discount yourself as someone who I can work through to reach out to others. You do not have to be perfect, but you do need to be willing to love as I love and to care about others as I care about all of My children.

Most of you have no idea of the personal connectivity that we have between us. In your mind, you would think that the impossible was happening when I urge you to extend yourself to aid another. If you get this type of inclination, act on it and know I am nudging you to take action. Do not think twice because that is when people come up with second thoughts, which tend to lead them away from their caring instincts. **Be as I am and look with compassion upon those whose lives are far more challenging than your own.**

> If you do not love and care for each other, there is no hope that your world will ever become truly civilized. Being civilized does not only mean remaining orderly and calm. Being civilized also means taking others into your hearts and having compassion for them and their situations. Being civilized means treasuring all other people, even those who may not be conducting themselves admirably. Being civilized does not mean being arrogant. It is just the opposite. Being civilized is the absence of any form of arrogance.

Now you know the preferable direction to take, and I advise you to begin right now, every one of you, to embrace My precepts and to display yourselves as the remarkable people that you are at the core of your being.

I am dismayed when My precious children feel inferior and less worthy or less important than others. You are imagining that other people are more valuable than you are when you feel inferior. You do not have to be a superior achiever in the physical world to be worthwhile. You are innately worthwhile because you are a part of Me.

Now you may be upset with yourself because you behaved shamefully, and I commend being upset with yourself when you know you could have, and should have, performed better than you did. What you need to understand is that the core of yourself is brilliant. The core of yourself contains My essence, which will never become extinguished.

I suggest that you acknowledge My presence within yourself at least twice a day, preferably when you awaken in the morning and then right before going to sleep at the end of your day. By connecting with My presence within you, it will eventually expand. Whether or not you go through this exercise, your connection with Me will always remain. However, if you wish to enrich your relationship with Me, those quiet times right before sleep and then when consciousness first comes back to you upon awakening in the morning are the best times. Once the world's demands pour forth, you may not think of Me again.

Now I am going to give you a little tip. When you set out to connect with My presence within you, clear your mind ahead of time. Do not expect success when you reach for Me amid the clutter of the day's activities until you become very skilled at controlling your thoughts and emotions. Initially, do not become discouraged when you do not receive a detectable response. If you continue to reach for Me with an open heart, sooner or later, you will realize My tingling presence becoming active within you.

I wish that every person on Earth would activate their innate yet currently dormant ability to realize My presence within themselves. When people detect that I am within them, it gives them an elevated feeling of peacefulness and well-being. Life's problems will still linger, but they will feel as if they are more in the background than right upfront and all-encompassing.

Most people bounce between their worries and their desires, which disrupts one's inner serenity. Everyone needs a firm support to rely on, as a constant in his or her life. Here I am, waiting for you to come to Me in the silence, within your pristine inner self.

I mentioned before that each of you is a part of Me and that we are eternally joined. Take advantage of the greatest gift that is available to you. Reach for Me. There is no separating layer between us.

You do not require a priest, a rabbi, a minister or any other religious authority to connect us. I am waiting for each of you to come to Me directly and to know Me personally. When you establish a close personal relationship with Me, you automatically tap into the greater part of yourself that lies at the core of your being. This is the genuine part of every person.

When you develop a direct personal relationship with Me, you become grounded in your wholeness. Your inner feelings about yourself become authentic, not puffed up, glamorized nor reduced, and you have no need for ego embellishment. You become serene and very content within yourself.

I want you to know that what I have just described is possible for each of you to achieve. You do not have to give up your individuality in any way. You just take on the completeness that is naturally yours when you set aside the divided self that almost all of you are accessing because you did not learn that the divided self is just the first stage of human development. Your next developmental goal is to unify your divided self with your innate grounding in My divine self, and you accomplish this by taking on My attributes and perceptions. This, My dear children, is why you are alive on Earth, battling your ego-driven actions and perceptions in order to evolve.

I am giving you all the information that you need in order to take that great leap forward into knowing yourself as being a treasured offspring of Mine. I know the difficulty that you have comprehending that you have the ability to be as I am. How I describe Myself is foreign to how human beings naturally express themselves, which may be unsettling to you initially. You do not usually think of Me as being within each and every one of you, and you do not know Me as being eager to have each and every one of you draw close to Me.

I do not push people away from Me, nor do I hold grudges for past mistakes. I am gracious, loving and accepting of all of My offspring regardless of their past errors. I invite you to put aside your past misperceptions about Me, about how I am, and what I require of each of you. I have been giving you a path to follow that is humane and character-building, which you have not received before in this detail.

Now I am going to make some demands. There are three requirements that I am setting forth for the entire human race. The sooner you take to heart that which I am giving you to accomplish and set forth to earn an A+ on this assignment, the greater will be the benefit delivered to humanity.

First, set aside disrespect for other people as something that is archaic and in its place, institute a universal commitment for treating others with concern, respect and tolerance.

Secondly, determine to act for the good of all and set aside your tendencies to be highly self-serving towards yourself and those who are most like you.

My third instruction is to set as your main goal in life, becoming closer to Me every day by demonstrating that you understand My teachings and are doing your best to implement My standards and behaviors as your own. If you want to please Me and draw close to Me, be as I am.

I do not accept excuses for poor performance when I have given you the benefit of being instructed directly by Me. You can make the excuse that figuring out how I really am is impossible because of inaccuracies passed down through religious teachings, and this excuse has merit. Do not look back. Look forward.

From now on, you no longer have an excuse for thinking that I am different than I truly am. Make an immediate determination to become as I am and then set out to instill My attitudes, perceptions and behaviors within yourself. Do not pass up this golden moment in time when you have an expanded opportunity to advance civilized behavior within yourself and within your communities all over the world.

CHAPTER SEVENTEEN

EARTH'S LOSS OF PATIENCE

As long as there are people on Earth, there will be conflict. Human nature has within it the need to be right even when wrong, the impulse of some to dominate and feel superior to others, and the most revolting characteristic of not valuing the preciousness of every other person. Many people feel that others are expendable, especially certain others, and have no inclination to open their hearts to them. When you look at someone on the street who is in an obviously desperate situation, what do you do? Does your heart fly open and ignite the urge to do whatever you can to help them, or do you think that something is innately wrong with them?

People turning their backs on other people is standard behavior on Earth. I bring up this subject to give you a bit of advice. In the years ahead, your human race will undergo severe tests and trials, the likes of which you cannot imagine from your perspective of here and now. Do not let your mind rebel and say, "Do not believe what you are reading." I caution you to take a deep breath, keep your mind open and read on. It is of paramount importance that each of you is informed ahead of time.

It is almost too late to prevent your planetary home's natural reaction to the negligent treatment she receives from humanity on a regular basis. Planet Earth has consciousness. Your planet is not an unfeeling object. She is an extension of Myself, which you are as well. I want you to honor and protect the planet, which you rely on to house, clothe and feed you, instead of counting on her to be there for you when you neglect to be there for her. You are takers of her gifts without showing her that you treasure her contributions to your well-being.

Earth has consciousness, as you do. I created your planet as I created you, as extensions of Myself into physical form. Yet, upon her surface, wars rage, weapons are exploded, and man's inability to cohabitate peacefully continues its display. It should come as no surprise that Earth is about to start heaving humanity off her surface. I have been gentle with you up until now to lead you to understand how deficient many of your typical behaviors are. Now it is time to convey what you will not want to hear.

Your seemingly patient planet is considering giving up on humanity. She has lost faith that humanity will ever cherish her, as she deserves to be cherished. She is keenly aware of humanity's violent tendencies, and she does not want to keep providing the backdrop for human beings to act out their displeasure with one another.

Do not think that your planet is without consciousness. Earth is a greater being than you have the capacity to comprehend. Your perception is limited and very self-centered. Human beings look upon themselves as being of maximum importance. They take possession of the land even as they disregard their responsibility to maintain its natural, pristine condition. Nearly everywhere you go on your planet, where human beings have gone before, you see disregard for her well-being.

The perception of your planet as being an inanimate object given to you to serve your needs is gravely flawed. Her intelligence far surpasses your own, and her wrath is about to be displayed as a lesson to inform humanity that she will no longer tolerate their destructiveness. I am giving you this warning so you will know how to interpret her wrath when she displays it.

Do not close this book thinking, "I do not want to read this." This is what people have been doing: looking the other way while assuming that damaging actions toward your planet will not amount to anything. You have exploded bombs upon her surface, some to test their efficacy and others to annihilate people.

You cannot get along with each other, you discount the value of other human beings and you certainly take for granted that your planet will be all right and continue to provide for you regardless of what you do to her. Do you think that I am exaggerating? Be realistic, and do not cover yourself in excuses for your behavior.

I have yet to explain how effective your conservation efforts have been. What little united effort has gone into methods of conservation, from recycling to utilizing more environmentally friendly farming practices, has been beneficial, but it is too little too late. Certain industries continue to use dangerous amounts of toxic chemicals in their manufacturing processes, and these chemicals make their way into the air you breathe, the food you eat and the clothes you wear. You are poisoning your bodies as you go along, living life as usual.

Higher population levels require more food production, housing, clothing and more transportation to deliver goods and services. Human beings' needs are increasing exponentially due to population expansion, as are the demands on your planetary supplier of those necessities.

You cannot turn back the clock to a time when there was plenty of room for population expansion. With the advent of more effective medical treatments, people are living longer, which means more demands for food, shelter and other necessities. The combination of longer lifespans and population expansions put a strain on planet Earth's ability to continue the unlimited generosity that she displayed in the past.

She seemed to have an endless supply of land and water resources with which to support humanity. It is not the same now. Booming populations place a drain on the natural resources that her populations require.

If your planet Earth were a long-distance runner, she would be running on a track that gets longer instead of shorter, and there would be no finish line. How would you like to keep running with no end in sight while ever-increasing numbers of people throw debris in your way? Her patience has nearly run out, and you will begin to have indications that she is rumbling with intent to remove many of you from your planetary home, which you have assumed will go on serving you regardless of how you treat her.

Many of you will pray to Me in the years ahead to stop the destruction that Earth will employ to remove excess populations from her surface. By then, it will be too late. Her forces of destruction will be raging, and she will not pull them back to appease irresponsible populations, who did not respect and appreciate her until she withdrew her commitment to offer them safe residence.

Your lack of commitment to the well-being of your planet will boomerang on you, and you will suffer mightily. There remains only a small window of opportunity for humanity to avoid the horrifying experience of helplessly standing by while calamities on Earth swallow up profound numbers of people.

Go ahead and tell yourself that what I am describing is not going to occur, that the Earth is safe and so are her populations. You have been clinging to fantasies by not believing what knowledgeable experts have been telling you for years. If you do not like what someone says, even if it is rational and research indicates that it is accurate, you naysay it, ridicule and disregard it.

You have debunked the early warnings and fallen even further behind. Your planet is becoming more and more irritated with humanity's avoidance of pulling back from fossil fuel usage and implementing every possible method of remediation in order to restore her intention to continue to house humanity upon her surface.

As it is now, your planet is planning to cast most of you off her surface in a series of maneuvers, which she can control, although her volatility usually churns under her surfaces, deep within the bowels of the Earth. You do not think of your planet as being able to orchestrate at will dynamic implosions and explosions, droughts, famines and massive flooding. You do not look at your planet and think that she is evaluating whether or not she will allow another year to go by without roaring at humanity in displeasure over their self-absorbed negligence.

It is readily apparent that you do not revere your planet, nor do you take all precautions to ensure that she will remain clean, healthy and viable. You do not think to do for her what you do for yourselves. You take care of your own body, but your actions repeatedly demonstrate that you do not sufficiently treasure and care for her physical manifestation.

You are like spoiled children who want, want, want and want, but it simply does not occur to you to give your very best to love, appreciate and care for the planet who gives you the opportunity to enjoy all her richness, beauty and vitality. Spoiled children usually do not get far in life because they do not put forth their best effort to become responsible adults. Spoiled children want everything handed to them without having to earn that which they receive. My perception is that most people on Earth are not sufficiently grateful for all their planet provides for them, while they take for granted that she will continue to provide as she has been.

My warning to residents of planet Earth is to become deeply involved in remediating the damage already done to the pristine quality of the land, the waterways, and the air and to stop adding to the burden of contamination that arises from negligent behaviors. Give up treating your planet Earth as a dumping ground for toxins, garbage and materials such as chemicals, which are detrimental to her viability. You cannot strip her lands, pollute her waters, drop bombs on her surface and think that you are taking good care of your planet. You cannot bring more children into the world than your planet is capable of providing for and still have ample accommodations for everyone who is already there.

You have had an irrational conviction that everything will be all right on Earth despite the obvious problems that are mounting. Do not continue to sell yourself a bill of goods that serves no constructive purpose and that you will later regret.

Later always seems to be far off in the distance, but every *later* turns out to be a *now*. Are you ready for your planet to upheave and toss from her surface millions of people in order to establish her dominance once again? Even if you and your family are not directly affected, how will you handle knowing that in certain places around the world, people are suffering terribly? People may feel separate from each other but humanity as a whole has a deep connection with one another.

You are living in a time of upcoming disastrous occurrences, yet, you may not have been aware of this until I informed you. Now that I have been giving you this education, you are more fully equipped to view your world's situation with a clearer vision. I suggest that you help the rest to gain the clarity that you are developing. All of humanity is in the same boat, and you need to pull together to keep it afloat, which will take teamwork and unheralded support for your planet.

Waste no time. Investigate all the ways people can pull together to support your planet, your local environments and each other. View yourselves as potential heroes who are on a mission to ensure that your planet continues to support her human populations. Get to work. Every household can contribute, and every household needs to contribute. A few people cannot carry responsibility for the rest. All must participate. There needs to be community organization from the grassroots level up.

Without shared commitment and people who are willing to step forward to organize the group effort, not much accomplishment will materialize. People tend to splinter and not pull together, so prepare for naysayers who put a drag on the community effort. Do not allow naysayers to trip you up or slow you down.

Organization is of imperative importance, along with cooperation. Do not be a Pollyanna thinking that everything will be all right, even if there is no deliberate effort put forth. Grassroots efforts have the ability to ignite the national will to protect the viability of your planet and the future of the human race upon this planet.

I could have withheld any mention of what lies ahead for humanity, but I would be doing you a disservice if I did not explain what is going to occur and why. Most people do not comprehend that Earth is becoming an unsafe place to live for a great many people. It is not My vengeance being unleashed against you that will be the cause. Simply put, the reason the Earth will roar back at humanity is to vent her rage and to diminish humanity's damaging impact upon her. If someone treats you disrespectfully, you take steps to distance yourself from him or her. Earth has similar instincts toward the human race.

If you think that your planet is without feelings, you are sorely mistaken. Do not her weather patterns display a wide range of emotions from sunny, calm happiness to violent displays of adverse conditions? She is not pleased with the human race's single-minded focus on themselves and their taking for granted that she will always be dependably supportive. The jig is up. She is drawing a line in the sand, and she is not going to budge.

In the years ahead, you will see the manifestation of what I am explaining. Your planet Earth is going to become crankier and crankier and, more than occasionally, mean and aggressive. This is just the beginning. After a while, if there is still an insufficient response to her need for better treatment, she will turn up the heat, and it will not be pleasant.

She will press humanity to consider her well-being over their desires, which so far humanity has been loath to do. She is going to press, and then press some more, and more and more. She is going to rile humanity with a vengeance and when she does, think about the opportunities that the human race decided not to take in order to preserve her well-being.

The onus is upon you because you have created over-population and the ever-widening drain on the Earth's natural resources. You have also created weaponry that is destructive to Earth's well-being, and you continuously bring about the desecration of the Earth's pristine environment. You plunder your planet's resources and always expect more to be available.

Picture yourself being planet Earth and seeing no end in sight to the misery inflicted upon you by human beings, and envision what you would do to protect yourself.

Your time of decision and action is at hand. If humanity does not swiftly pull together to reverse the damage done and implement strict standards that will protect your planet, you will begin to see a decrease in your world's population brought about by your planet's fury. If you think that I am exaggerating to frighten you into taking protective action to safeguard your planetary residence, you are right, and you are wrong.

I am not putting enough emphasis on the extent of the horror that you will live through. I am not giving you all of that to swallow at this time. I am doing My best to guide you into realizing that how life has been in the past is not a valid indication of how it will be in the future.

Proceed at your own risk, and do not pray to Me to save you from the destruction your planet will produce. This is your moment of opportunity to save yourselves from proceeding to create an intolerable situation for your planet. She is not without intelligence and judgment, and she has the right to act to protect herself. Why would I want to influence planet Earth to continue to provide for a species that dishonors her and refuses to take sufficient action to preserve her integrity after receiving warnings of the consequences?

One of humanity's evolutionary goals has been to learn to pull together to accomplish that which is necessary for everyone to thrive. There are those who devote themselves to humanitarian causes and those who devote themselves to the preservation of your planet. I commend all of these enlightened people, and I am telling the rest of you to become as they are.

Join their efforts and do your best to reconfigure what life on Earth is like for the underprivileged populations in your own backyards and throughout the world.

Do not be delinquent and leave it to other people to perform good deeds for others. Pitch in and participate in aiding those who need to rely on the assistance of others to come to their rescue.

Your planet also requires you to come to her rescue. You can help rescue your planet by changing your ways. I admonish you to stop thinking of her as ever-providing in a selfless way. She requires attention immediately.

Ponder the fact that what human beings choose to do to their planet determines the future viability of the human race upon her surface. If there were no human beings, your planet would be in pristine condition. You are making a huge mistake if you think that you can continue to trash your planet and not have to pay the price for your unevolved practices.

What do you value? What makes you feel complete? I advise you to take the trip inside, to know yourself in more depth than superficially. I invite you to move close to Me, welcoming Me into your mind and your heart as a permanent resident. I am close to every one of you, waiting for you to notice My Presence. Very few do, yet all of you could. I am waiting for you, patiently waiting for you to detect My Presence. I am not going to force Myself upon anyone. I want you to come to Me and welcome Me into your mind and your heart.

Have you had the experience of not noticing someone who was next to you until you heard them speak? I suggest that you teach yourself to recognize My presence within you. I speak to My children; however, only rarely do they notice because they are not tuned in to My presence. Only if you tune in to My presence will you enliven our connectivity enough for you to begin to detect My outreach to you. Here are a few simple steps that you can take to build the bridge of energetic connectivity between you and Me.

The first step is to know within your heart and your mind that I am reachable and that you are acceptable to Me as you are. I do not judge and find some to be unworthy. Know that you and all others are in My heart already. I recognize your strengths and your weaknesses.

The second step is for you to cast off instinctive or deliberate behaviors that do not honor the preciousness of all humanity. Support the well-being of other people and avoid obstructing any person's well-being. Develop determination to be a positive force for good at all times and under all conditions. Recognize every other person as your beloved sister or brother, and cherish him or her in your mind and your heart.

The third step is to develop an attitude of loving and caring. People have the ability to love and respect even those they do not particularly admire. One can train themself to love and respect people who do not have admirable qualities. Being gracious to all is the best way to interact with others.

I am a conscious, active presence within each of you even when you do not perceive My presence. I do not interfere. I witness your struggles and your victories. Your drama of life on Earth is revealed to Me. You perceive your personal snippet of experience, whereas I have an awareness of what each one of you is going through. Do not ever feel that you are not near and dear to Me, My beloveds.

I want you to know this about Me. I am patient and forgiving. My love is unconditional, and I do not keep track of all of your misdeeds. Some religious teachings have misrepresented how I am. Do not be fearful of judgment and damnation but do take the opportunity now to evaluate your perceptions and behaviors based on what I am teaching you. Keep yourself from going in the wrong direction when the right direction is discernable.

Do the right thing. Go forward in your life with an eye toward self-improvement, which is the most worthwhile goal you can pursue. Do not dawdle and waste your time in the classroom of life. Instead, make this lifetime count as a big positive in your forward progress to understand and refine your attitudes and behavior. Take charge of how you construct your life in order to enhance your evolutionary development.

CHAPTER EIGHTEEN
TAKE ACTION NOW

My children, I have my loving arms around every one of you, although there seems to be a veil separating us from each other. The veil is only on your part of the viewing, not on My part. If you saw yourselves as I see you, you would clearly identify your strengths and your shortcomings.

I have been highlighting your shortcomings and encouraging you to face them straight on before they become more pronounced. When a weed starts growing in your garden, it will expand in size and be more difficult to extract if you do not pull it out right away. All of you, with only a few exceptions, have been living with weeds in the garden of yourself.

I am taking it upon Myself to educate you directly in order to set you on the right path of evolving yourself to become as I am. I am helping you to identify the weeds in the garden of your self-presentation. I encourage you to extract them before their roots deepen and become more anchored into your self-expression.

Replace your weeds with blooming flowers of gracious, loving concern for the wellbeing of all people. Tap into the side of your self-expression that you inherited from Me. I will support your every endeavor to model your feelings, attitudes and actions to match Mine.

Every effort you make to pattern yourself after Me will produce a positive effect. When you are watchful, you will more likely notice the subtle improvements that filter into your self-expression. Other people will notice, as well, and express more warmth and genuine caring towards you. You will be appealing to others and will feel relaxed and comfortable in your own shoes without trying to be impressive. Genuineness is a most appealing trait to establish within yourself.

I am talking to you as a child of Mine, as each of you truly is. I want you to reform yourself to exhibit My characteristics as your own. If everyone in your world reflected their linage, all people would be gracious and kind-hearted, supportive of the well-being of all others without exception, and fastidiously safeguarding your precious planet Earth. If you grew up from infancy in such a world as I describe, it would be natural for you to place protective arms around planet Earth and each other.

I do not want you to fumble your way forward, which is what you have been doing. Fumbling your way forward is not going to improve living conditions for masses of individuals who are struggling to get by in substandard living conditions. Nor will it cleanse your waterways and oceans. The time has come for every person to take joint responsibility for restoring the pristine nature of your planet and creating civility between all people. You need to wake up to the destructive forces at play and realize that you are living during the time of Earth's deterioration, adding to the problems without conscious recognition of your culpability in causing them.

I encourage you to base your actions on this one directive that I give to all of My children. Do unto others that which you would have others do unto you. If you followed this directive, there would be no cheating and no underhandedness in human relationships. I suggest that you picture yourself as the oceans. Would you allow yourself to be utilized as a toxic dumping ground? Then picture yourself as the sky. Would you allow pollution rising up from landmasses to choke off your ability to remain clean and pure?

Think of yourself as a poor person who has little or no assets. You see other people spending money on lavish things while you cannot afford to feed and clothe your family or yourself. You have sunk so far down that, given your circumstances, there is no feasible way up for you. Your heart aches for your spouse and children, and you feel ashamed that you cannot adequately provide for them.

I see all of you as equal to each other. Try telling a millionaire who hoards his excess that the impoverished person requesting money on the side of the road is his sister or his brother. Try telling a strong, athletic person that the broken-down sick-looking person is his sibling in the sight of God. Try telling a rich person that their good fortune blesses him or her when they utilize their good fortune to aid people in need. The best use for one's good fortune is sharing it with others to pull them up out of life's difficulties and give them some breaks in life that have been unattainable to them.

Every person lives a great number of lifetimes. I want you to have the full human experience and every opportunity to evolve yourselves. One lifetime cannot give you the full spectrum of life situations that you need in order to refine your attitudes and behaviors.

I would like to point out that many world servers have incarnated at this time. World servers are people who have long since graduated from the schoolhouse of Earth, but their devotion to helping humanity evolve brings them back repeatedly to play a part in the education of people on Earth. Blessed individuals such as Mother Theresa, Reverend Martin Luther King and many others, whose names you would not recognize, devoted their lifetimes to demonstrating loving acceptance of all people, especially those who were downtrodden.

Humanity needs heroes to take the sand out of people's eyes, better enabling them to perceive the preciousness of every person. Clear seeing people see all as equals. They do not use wealth, status or position as the determinant of worthwhileness. Wealth, status or position does not ensure a more advanced person. Honesty, integrity, humbleness and generosity are more meaningful as indicators of superior qualities in an individual.

Every person needs to take all others into their hearts and minds. Love and accept all people unconditionally, even those who are offensive to you. There are reasons why people are the way they are. Everyone is a mix of their true authentic self, their imprinting as a child, and their self-expression as a product of lifetimes of evolutionary development. Within each person is a combining of that which they brought in with them from other lifetimes, the impact of their home and family situation when they were young, and their progression in evolutionary development that they have achieved thus far in this lifetime.

When you think of yourself only as you are now, you are missing the greater picture of the whole entirety of your lifetimes. Each person has undergone an endless number of life experiences on planet Earth. Although your common goal is to elevate your attitudes, actions and behaviors, most people experience more of a yo-yo effect of up and down rather than an airplane effect of only going up. Some lifetimes display more advancement than others do. Almost all people experience lifetimes when their evolutionary development stagnated or declined instead of rising up to a higher level of self-actualization.

The evolutionary process is, for the most part, slow but very enriching. People often learn more when they inch along, not setting goals that are too ambitious for them to achieve than if they shoot for the moon but fail to launch. The problem with the slow evolutionary progress is that planet Earth is losing ground in her struggle to maintain Earth as a viable planet for humanity to occupy. This puts pressure on the timeline for humanity to implement sufficient environmental safety precautions, which most of humanity does not acknowledge as being necessary.

It is business as usual for the greater part of humanity, as the smaller group of knowledgeable and concerned people try to muster a unified effort to protect the well-being of your planetary residence. Some people are dedicated to advancing this effort. Other people sit on their hands, ignoring the rational alarms sounded by the concerned and knowledgeable forward thinkers.

In order for Earth to remain a viable planet for future generations, participation is universally required of all residents of planet Earth to do everything in their power to reverse the current disregard for her well-being. If humanity turns its back on Mother Earth, she will roar back with a vengeance. It would not take much for your planet to lose her balance and begin to wobble, significantly creating danger in certain populated areas, which would be significantly unsettling for the people affected. This will be her announcement that she is no longer going to coddle humanity until they grow up and become responsible residents of planet Earth.

You may think that what you are reading is a script for a horror movie. You are already living the horror movie on Earth by ignoring the extreme need to safeguard your planet and to implement improved ethical standards of interactions with all people. Bumping along as you have been is not going to work anymore. I urge you to be rational, realistic and eager to put far more into elevating your perceptions and behaviors and into preserving your natural environment than you have ever been before. You are tempting fate by not taking swift and decisive action to protect your planet in every conceivable way.

Now that I sounded that alarm for you, I will turn in another direction. I want everyone to take an inventory of his or her strengths and weaknesses. Parents pass along predispositions to behave one way or another. Their children have the choice of mimicking their parents, one or the other, or both, but they also have the option to reject duplicating any behavior, which falls into the categories of demeaning, physically or psychologically crushing, neglectful or indecent. Parents have responsibilities for their children's well-being beyond feeding, clothing and housing them. Parents' responsibilities go much further than that.

When parents are cruel to their son or daughter, they send two messages. The first message is that the parent does not care if he or she is hurting their offspring. The second message is that the parent has rejected the son or daughter. Both of these messages hit hard and destroy a child's sense of security. An adult who would have been dynamic and self-assured had they not been cruelly treated as a child tends to limp along during their life, being less secure and maintaining a fearful undertone, which holds them back from achieving up to their potential.

Do not think that harm inflicted upon a child does not matter. Would you take a hammer and pound it on your new car? Some people are more protective of their automobiles than they are of their own children.

The Golden Rule states, "Do unto others as you would have others do unto you." Picture yourself as you were when you were a young child and as a teenager. How did your parents relate to you, and how did each of them influence your self-esteem? Now review yourself. Do you notice yourself falling into some of the same negative traits that one or both of your parents displayed toward you? It is common for people abused as children to mistreat their own children. The cycle often repeats.

Knowing that this stream of behavior tends to continue should sound alarms for parents mistreated as children to be especially caring in their interactions with their own children. Be sure that you honor, respect and care for your children and that you do not burden them with disrespect or lack of caring.

Now I have another question. How do you feel when someone is deliberately disrespectful to you? When you have high self-esteem, you are more likely to disregard the episode letting it pass without any significant disturbance on your part.

A mistreated child's self-esteem withers, and then that child carries their silent burden throughout their lifetime. No matter how successful they are in adulthood, they are never completely free of nagging inner distress associated with low self-esteem. A child's self-esteem thrives when they receive unconditional love and support from their family. Solid self-esteem flourishes from being positively nurtured and respected throughout childhood.

I am in favor of people consciously determining whether to bring new life into your world. As already stated, your planet is overpopulated. In many parts of your world, a reduction in population growth would enhance Earth and humanity's well-being. It is nearly too late to halt overpopulation's devastating effects upon humanity.

Too many people are already present, placing a strain on comfortable living conditions for a great number of the world's residents. Your world's populations are watching as if in a movie theater to see what happens next. However, in a movie theater, the film concludes, and all those who attended the movie return to their safe homes.

Your planet is not as interested in keeping the status quo as you are. You may be willing to overlook disastrous occurrences upon Earth as long as those occurrences do not yield a direct impact upon you. You perceive in terms of *today* and *me* instead of *tomorrow* and *we*.

Consider your planet as a boat and humanity as the passengers on that boat. The passengers are enjoying their ride and not anticipating that there is about to be a preventable calamity. They are enjoying their boat ride to such an extent that they are not aware that they have taken on too many passengers to ensure the safety of the boat. The boat is getting wobbly with the increased population load, and food is about to run out because there are too many people needing to be fed. The boat's passengers wish that occupancy had been limited to a practical number of people so they would be comfortable and well provided for.

Would you like to be a passenger on that boat? You already are a passenger on that boat. You refuse to plan and restrict while you enjoy yourselves today, ignoring the need to make rational prearrangements for tomorrow. Proceed at your own risk and know that you are bringing down upon yourselves tomorrow's catastrophes, which you could have prevented.

You may ignore My effort to educate you, or it may spark men and women everywhere to remove their blindfolds and get ready to do the heavy lifting. The first wave of responders to rational self-preservation of humanity must begin immediately. Do not sit back and wait for the politicians to take the first steps. They will be looking behind their backs to determine if taking as strong a stance as is necessary will be politically detrimental to their reelection.

Politicians sway with public opinion. The public actually holds the reins in their hands. I will be your partner guiding you if you care enough about the future of your planet to follow My instructions.

The first step is to be firm in your commitment to protect your planet's well-being, so firm that you are willing to tolerate adjustments in the way you do things. People have varying degrees of rigidity within them. Some cling to the status quo as if they were in danger of losing their life if they budged. Others slip and slide all over the place, championing one cause only until the next one comes along. Your planet Earth needs all of you to make an ironclad commitment to her well-being. How willing are you to stand tall in your protection of your planet?

Let us discuss morals and ethics. Moral, ethical people hold themselves to high standards of conduct. They quiz themselves about the appropriateness of the decisions they make. They would rather catch themselves before taking a wrong step than going back and attempting to correct it after the fact.

Where do you stand on going out of your way to safeguard your planet? Does this subject bore you because you do not think it is as much of a problem as doomsayers suggest? Do you think that this is not going to affect you during your lifetime?

Your planet Earth needs you to stand up for her right now, not later, nor never. When your house is on fire, do you delay summoning assistance? Do you wait to see if the fire goes out on its own? How many fires suddenly extinguish themselves?

I anoint every person on Earth as your planet's protector. Earth needs every one of you, especially the younger generations, to take personal action to secure the safety and viability of your planetary provider. Treat your planet as you would prefer to be treated if you were planet Earth. Imagine yourself being a mother or father to children who disregard your well-being. Sadly, this is what planet Earth endures now.

Do not remain one of the masses of people who holds back on taking every possible step to cleanse and reinvigorate the viability of your precious planet Earth. Full charge ahead! Become Earth's protector. Do away with toxic chemicals on the land. Do not use waterways as chemical dumps. Do not revere moneymaking activities over every person's responsibility to cherish and protect your planet, Earth. You will be protecting your own linage, as well as future generations.

Every person has a role to play, so do not excuse yourself from wholehearted participation in rescuing planet Earth from human disregard. If Earth were without her human populations, your planet would not require assistance. She would thrive. Humanity is not a necessity for planet Earth.

It is up to current generations to determine the future of humanity on Earth. Nero watched as Rome burned. Are you ready to watch as your planet loses her determination to support humanity as residents upon her surface? I have warned you enough to inspire you to dislodge from your do-nothing attitudes. Just remember that you are the cause of Earth's temperamental actions. Do not point your finger at any other cause.

Before I conclude this missive to you, My children, I am giving you every benefit that I can to steer you in a more wholesome direction. I am extending Myself, as your Creator God, to infuse you with My palpable presence at this exact point. If you do not detect My energetic presence, remain still, calm and patient. Sense a delicate, sweet, light, tingling presence throughout your body. Your head and your legs may detect My presence more strongly than the rest of your body. Many of you will begin to feel sleepy and have a difficult time keeping your eyes open. You will be sensing the blessing of My presence overshadowing you.

Now I want you to deliberately strengthen My presence within you by saying to yourself, "Creator God and I are one. Creator God and I are one." Every time you say, "Creator God and I are one," My presence will become more deeply rooted within you. If you are driving a car, you had better pull over to the side of the road before beginning this connecting process. Your energetic frequency may become too elevated to think or react clearly enough to drive a car.

Practice this procedure that I am giving you, especially in times of hardship or despair. If you concentrate on My presence within you and do not allow anything else to intrude, I will partner with you to overcome anguish or despondency. You are never alone. I am always with you, but it is up to you to heighten our connectivity. I patiently wait for you to expand your experience of My presence within yourself.

The energetic response that I will give you attests to the reality of My presence becoming expanded within yourself. No one other than yourself is necessary for you to ignite the ever-present relationship between us. Intermediaries cannot do for you that which you can do for yourself. You are the only one who can create personal closeness between us.

Picture yourself as My offspring. Do not look in the mirror at your human body and think that your body is who you are. Your body is perishable, but you are not.

> You will always continue to exist in your spirit form, which is what animates your physical body. Your spirit form is on an adventure to experience the physical world and its delusions and to rise above the delusions to connect with the essence of your being.

Human beings do not easily awaken to their authentic identity. They focus on the fabrications of their ego and their physical appearance. The combination of ego expressions and physical appearances cannot lead a person to recognize themself as divine offspring. The arrow points the wrong way.

The right way to touch into the divine inner self, which exists within every person, is to forget about the ego and all that attunes you to the physical world. Do not think of your list of accomplishments or failures as determining who you are. Consider yourself an innate part of your Creator God who greatly loves you, as well as every other person. You are parts of God, but you do not identify yourselves as such because you are only in touch with your exterior presentation and not in touch with the core of your being, which is the spark of divinity that ignited you into creation.

If you took off your body, you would still exist. You do not require a physical body to exist as a separate and unique individual. The selfness that is you continues to experience on and on and on. It never becomes extinguished or abandoned. My presence within everyone stays intact even when a person does not reflect My values and standards. When one allows their ego free reign to scoop up all that it can, they have withdrawn from allowing their god-self within to shine through as it would if they were attuned to My presence within them.

I hope you comprehend what I am saying. If not, go over these explanations and think about them until they make sense to you. I understand that you are not used to seeing yourselves in any other way than in your current physical form. You are more used to criticizing other people than taking a realistic assessment of your own attitudes and behaviors. This may be the biggest obstacle to humanity's evolutionary advancement.

I am giving you notice that time is running out for the human race to thrive upon your planet. Misery lies ahead as population expansion places more and more strains on your Earth's ability to provide as she has in the past. I am telling you once again that the human race is sitting on the brink of destruction while behaving as if the problems will erase themselves without humanity doing much to halt and reverse the tragedy.

The tragic loss of Earth's unspoiled atmosphere, waters and land is leaving your planet with no alternative than to eject people off her surface. You know how miserable a flea-infested animal feels and how the only relief for that animal lies in the elimination of the fleas. People are not fleas, but they are sucking the lifeblood out of planet Earth's ability to support humanity as it has in the past.

> I am willing to support your planet's stability for a while longer if nations around the world work cooperatively to employ strict environmental restoration regulations. This will take unity of purpose, agreement on what needs to happen, cooperative effort and worldwide enforcement of the agreed-upon plan of action.

If a worldwide plan of action takes hold and becomes implemented by most of the world's communities with determination to halt and then reverse the battering that your planet is constantly receiving, I will give you a time extension to work on these efforts. In addition, inhabitants of Earth must take personal responsibility to protect their planet by restricting population expansion. These issues go hand in hand, and both must be reconciled.

Now, if you think that focusing on these two issues is too much of a hassle for you to go through, do not assume that the alternative is the easy way out. My beloved children, you have no easy way out. Only if you face the music now with gusto will your children and your grandchildren have a pleasant and supportive planetary home to enjoy in the decades ahead.

You can be gloomy and disturbed, or you can power up and get after the restoration job that you have ahead of you. Fear, self-pity or delay will not move you toward your goal of redeeming your planet's ability and determination to continue to support its populations. Your planet needs a speedy indication that humanity is taking responsibility for their planet's well-being.

If My warning evokes an insufficient response, you will be forced to swallow a bitter pill of your own creation. You may feel safe and secure at this moment but do not take this as a guarantee of how you will feel when you finally decide to forge ahead to protect your planet and then realize that you are too late. As I have already stated, it is nearly too late right now. Your window of opportunity to be able to reverse the already disastrous condition that engulfs your planet is no longer wide open. It has been closing at a swifter and swifter pace, nearly squeezing you out of having any say in the matter.

The element of time allows you to cut short the difficulties that confront human beings. Living in a human body comes with requirements that must be satisfied, and because of the time limitation of a human lifespan, there is a point when the struggle to maintain the body mercifully concludes. You may pass from your body grateful that you lived a full life, or you may pass prematurely because of Earth's vindictive attitude towards humanity's disregard for her well-being.

I have nearly given up hope that a vast number of you will rise to make your voices heard, your influence felt and your determination to do all you can to preserve your planet's safety take hold amidst disinterested populations. As I demonstrated in these chapters, I know humanity well, and I see their disinterest in doing all they can to preserve their planet in the pristine condition that she deserves to enjoy. Those, who turn away from their obligation to their planet, will be those who cry the loudest for Me to come and save them from suffering the repercussions of their wrong thinking and failure to act when they should have. I will stand aside and allow your planet to purge herself of human malfeasance.

I love you, and I want the best for you. I give you a wide berth to design your personal self-expression. It is up to you to decide whether to take a slow and bumpy evolutionary path or to jump right in and get to work. It is your choice to determine if you will gravitate toward following the high road or if you choose to dawdle and delay advancing your evolutionary progress. There is no deadline. Creation goes on and on beyond what your human minds would be able to comprehend if it were all explained.

Your lives are challenging even when they seem rather quiet and ordinary. All people are being tested throughout their lives, even when it looks like some sail along without much drama or trauma. Those blessed souls who suffer tremendous difficulty may appear to be weak and not extraordinary through the eyes of their fellow human beings, but that is not how I see them. Especially those who walk the path of being downtrodden and not sufficiently aided by those who could extend assistance deserve release from their body without having to continue their extraordinary distress. For those people, exiting from their physical body brings blessed relief, although, from the human point of view, their loss of life constitutes the worst thing that could happen to them.

The worst thing that can happen to an individual is for them to devolve instead of evolving during their lifetime. Your lifetimes are opportunities to climb the evolutionary ladder as high as you can, thereby guaranteeing that when you return for your next physical life experience, you will reenter human experience at a more advanced level. If you waste your opportunity to develop more evolved perceptions, attitudes and actions during this incarnation, you will disappoint yourself. Your goal is to become as I am, which can only happen when you strive to take on My traits as your own.

There is no way to get around having to accurately face oneself and take direct action to clip off one's unevolved attitudes and actions, and to implant My traits and characteristics in place of them. Once you decide to imitate Me, you will find that it really is a simple matter to become as I am. I urge you to follow the high road in life.

Learn from Me and take My explanations to heart. If you had known all along how I am and you had seen other people modeling the high road, taking it would have been second nature to you. You would have marched in step with other enlightened beings.

Now you must swiftly catch up to where you would have been had you been given the head start of experiencing My traits modeled to you since you were young. Embrace My instructions and set out to encourage the rest of humanity to follow in your footsteps as you follow in Mine.

I hereby call all of you who read what I have to say and deeply resonate with the information that I am conveying. I invite each of you to join with Me. Together we need to influence people all over the world to become more attuned to the precarious situation that has developed on Earth and the need for devoted efforts by people of all nations to band together to preserve the Earth's safety and integrity for the new generations that will come along.

Now is the time to make an upstanding commitment to future generations that they will inherit a planetary home, which has been well cared for, and which is capable of supplying the needs of her human populations, whose growth has declined in numbers due to fastidious attention to vastly slowing population expansion. **Act now to protect the future of the human race upon planet Earth.**

If you value what you learned, please submit a review at Amazon.com

DIVINE RESOURCES FOR ALL

The best way to live is to keep in mind what you are here to accomplish. Go beyond the typical aspirations. God Talks to All of Us, enlightens you on how to live your best life. This book's companion What It Is Like to Die and What Comes After will prepare you to move into the higher dimensions after your death, no matter the circumstances. To discover more about available resources on how to evolve, now and after death, visit DivineResourcesForAll.com.

SHARE YOUR THOUGHTS AND HELP OTHERS DISCOVER THE INSIGHTS IN THIS BOOK

If you gained value and enjoyed God Talks, we would love you to pop online and leave a review on Amazon or Goodreads. Reviews help other people find and enjoy independent books.

For Amazon:

1. Search "God Talks to All of Us" in the search bar
2. Click on the book page
3. Scroll down to where it says Customer Reviews
4. Click on Write a Customer Review

Note: You'll need to be logged in to your Amazon account and Amazon requires you to spend at least $50 per year to be able to leave a review

For Goodreads:
1. Search "God Talks to All of Us" in the search bar
2. Click on the book page that comes up under the search bar
3. Click on the box under the cover image and change to Read
4. A pop-up box will appear for you to leave a review
5. Once you've typed in your review and left a star rating, click save.

Kay would love to hear how this book has impacted you. To share your story, please do get in touch via DivineResourcesForAll.com.

God Talks to
All of Us,

Thoughts to
Keep in Mind

Practice and Evolve

Presented By
Kay Mielenz

This booklet contains selected excerpts from God Talks to All of Us to support your daily endeavor to evolve your attitudes and behaviors. Keep in mind that even with a firm desire to advance your personal traits, your path will bring both successes and failures. Be patient with yourself and remain dedicated. Enjoy your feelings of well-being as they multiply.

You can find these books on Amazon, from DivineResourcesForAll.com and in all good bookstores.

What It Is Like to Die and What Comes After demonstrates what happens to people after they die. Deceased people tell their stories, which deliver insight into how to die with the assurance that one will easily transfer into a desirable afterlife. This book also contains messages to loved ones from those who are deceased. *What It Is Like to Die and What Comes After* is a must-read for anyone who wants to have documentation about what occurs when physical life ends.

Discover:
- Core insights that will prevent you from becoming stuck between this world and the next.
- Common pitfalls after dying and how to navigate them.
- Relief knowing there is a place for everyone within the heavens, even those who lived misguided lifetimes.
- Transformative knowledge that will allow you to face death without fear, by clearly understanding how to navigate what comes next.
- How to avoid after-life regrets.

Made in the USA
Columbia, SC
27 November 2021

49673217R00166